T1

Dedication

First and foremost, this book is dedicated to:

My Brothers, Eric and Brad Smith

My Sister, Staci

My Mom and Dad, Joyce and Sam (George)

My Daughters, Vannessa Leigh and Kellie Anne

My Wife, Paula

It is also dedicated to all of my brothers and sisters in the military. To those who gave, and would give, their last full measure of devotion in service to their country.

Smith

About the Author

Gregg was born in September of 1973 and was raised in the Eugene-Springfield, Oregon area. He has two brothers, twelve and ten years older; and a sister, about 16 months older. He has two daughters, Vannessa Leigh and Kellie Anne, who are the pride and joy of his life and the inspiration for his continued improvement in life.

During his family's many moves when he was younger, he attended Goshen Elementary for Kindergarten, Moffitt Elementary for 1st-2nd grade, Elizabeth Page Elementary for part of 3rd grade, Washington Elementary for the other part of 3rd – 5th grade, James Monroe Middle School for 6th -8th grade, and Henry D. Sheldon High School for 9th -12th grade. His college years were spent at Regis University in Denver, Colorado where he received a Bachelor of Science in Business Administration with a specialization in Marketing and an MBA in Operations/Project Management.

He now resides in Cheyenne, Wyoming with his wife Paula and younger daughter Kellie. Since he has always enjoyed music, he wanted to make it a point to share that love with his family. He believes that if a person has a passion in life, they will be happier if they can share it.

School has always been fun for him, and writing has always come relatively easy. It was suggested that he write down events that came to his mind while in the military to try and make sense of how his mind worked. Through those notes, the idea of putting them together into a book was born.

For his brothers and sisters in arms who have struggled because they are misunderstood, or for those who cannot get help, this book is for them.

Preface

There are times in everyone's life when they look back at the decisions they made to get them to where they are at that moment in time. The triggers for these thoughts could be sounds, smells, views, or a word said by a stranger in passing.

My look back was triggered when my daughter asked me what the medals in my shadow-box were for. She pointed to my Purple Heart and simply said, "Daddy got hurt?" Apparently, my wife had told her a little about the medals already.

As I talked about the medals and the uniform decorations in my other shadow-box, I remembered the instances that led me to receive each of the items I was telling her about. She was not even three years old yet, but she could read the pain, sorrow, and happiness in my eyes as I spoke.

I regret certain inconsequential decisions I have made, like staying up too late when I had to get up early the next day. Decisions I NEVER regret are the ones that made me the man I am today; a father, a son, a brother, a husband, a friend, a soldier.

There is a saying that hung in every office I have had since I joined the Army in June of 1997. It reminded me of the roots of who I was as a soldier, and who I was protecting:

"I am the American Soldier. For the American people, my family, my sons to come – I carry on. Born of explorers, colonists, hunters in deer skins; schooled in the wilderness fighting for our continent – I carried on for the rights of man. Wherever I was needed, whenever I was called, I stood and delivered. I came through. I was America on the march. And now today here I

come again, marching again at the same old job – same old brand new job – marching again with all free men. I am the ring of steel around democracy; the ramparts that you sing about; I am the Citizen Soldier; the Nation in Arms. I am the eyes of the cannon, the marching refrain, the brains of the tank, the nerves of the plane, the heart of the shell. I am the Liberty Bell, the salt of our youth. I am the fighting man of every outpost from Alaska to Hawaii to Korea and beyond; from Panama to Puerto Rico to Iceland and beyond. Whatever the need – for the spirit of Liberty, for the future we're making – I, the American Soldier, am the shield." – Author Unknown.

Our chosen life

Chapter 1

Going through school I was a happy person. I did well in school, lived and breathed music, and had some very pretty girlfriends. My plan was to go to college after high school and get a job teaching or something. After graduation I got lazy and that all changed.

At the time, I had never even considered joining any branch of the military, even though many members of my family had. Closest to me, my Grandfather Walter Miller was in the Army Infantry and my Uncle Keith Miller was in Air Force Communications. I had heard some of the stories from both of them about World War II and Vietnam respectively. They obviously did not paint a pretty picture about life in the military during wartime, and those images stuck with me and caused me steer away from the Army after high school.

I spent a lot of time with the younger of my two older brothers and my sister. The closeness of family made life appear happy and fulfilled, and for the most part is was. In hindsight, uneventful is not life, it's getting by. I got by from the time I graduated until August 11th, 1995. That date became the crossroads that would prove to change my life, and my family, forever.

I woke up around nine in the morning that day and went upstairs. My grandparents, Walter and Audrey, were visiting from Iowa. My mom was upstairs visiting with my grandparents. My dad, Sam, was at work. My sister, Staci, was living elsewhere. My brother, Brad, was living at home at the time.

My grandparents had asked Brad to take a look at their seatbelt because it was having issues and not retracting as it should. Brad and

I went outside to take a look at it. We tried for about a half an hour but could not get it fixed. Brad was always the first to stand up for the weaker person or to try and help someone. Even at ten years older than myself, we were the closest of any two people in my family. I had a new girlfriend at the time so I wanted to spend a little time with her. My brother had some things to do so we told my grandparents we couldn't fix the seatbelt and went on our separate ways. I often think back to that day and question my decision. If I would have stayed there, or if I had gone with my brother to run his errands, would it have made a difference? Almost daily, I beat myself up about that.

The rest of the day went like any other summer day. It was eighty-five degrees that day, which is hot for Eugene, Oregon, so we went to the mall and then to the movies that afternoon. After the movies were over, we did the 1950's cruising the gut thing in our cars and hanging out with our friends at certain convenience stores. The "circuit," as we called it, was created when the city of Eugene banned cruising due to crime. Cruising took me back to when I was in high school. It was a fond memory that I have that I like to hold close to me. It takes about two and a half hours to complete the whole thing if you don't stop.

The movie got out around five and we went to the circuit. We stopped a few times for gas, food, and to talk to people then went on our way. After going through the circuit a couple times I dropped my girlfriend and my friends off at their houses. By the time I got home it was about eleven at night. The whole time I was out and about, I was thinking that I should have stayed home to spend a little time with my grandparents while they were visiting from Iowa, but I was a normal guy who just wanted to spend time with his girlfriend. I figured that I would have all the time in the world to see my family.

My first clue that something was wrong was that the lights were on when I pulled up to the house. The second clue was that my parent's car was not in the driveway. Considering it was a weekday, this was very unusual. I was worried that something had happened to one of my grandparents, but they both appeared in the doorway as I walked up to the house.

My grandmother told me to come in and sit down, and that she had something to tell me. They were clearly upset and emotional about something. My fear at that point was that something happened to one of my parents. She proceeded to tell me that my parents were at the hospital. The words I'll never forget came out of her mouth next, "something has happened to Brad."

At that point, I was in trance mode. They told me that my parents had asked them to tell me to stay home, but I couldn't. All I could say was, "where are they at?" They said that my parents had been gone for a few hours and that they would probably be home anytime. I kept asking where they were and after about ten minutes they finally told me. I ran out to my car and took off down the street.

Once I got onto the interstate that led to the hospital I sped up and drove at about a hundred to a hundred and ten miles an hour to the emergency room. When I walked in, there were no people in the waiting room. I walked up to the nurse in charge and asked where my family was. She took out the log book and started flipping to that night's log entries. She asked what the name was and I told her "Brad Smith." The other nurse at the station looked at her as she slowly closed the book. As it closed, the sound of the pages falling felt like I was being slapped. When the cover fell shut, it felt like my heart stopped. She looked at me and told me to wait in the hall for the hospital Chaplain. I knew at that point that I was too late. He had been shot six times. As I stood there waiting I went into a kind of dazed shock. The hospital called my parents, who I had passed on the way to the hospital, and told them that I was there. They agreed that the Chaplain should tell me what happened and assess whether or not I should be kept there to wait for a ride. I spent about a half an hour sitting there and regaining my composure. I was OK to drive so they let me take myself home.

I learned later that my mom and dad had stopped by my sister Staci's house on the way home from the hospital. When my sister answered the door and saw my parent's standing there she just said, "Oh no, this can't be good."

My dad called Eric while I was on my way home. When my brother answered the phone he only heard five simple words, "this is Dad, Brad's dead."

Reality really hadn't set in for me at the hospital or even during the drive home. That changed when I got home. My family always knew how we felt about each other, but we were never particularly huggy. My parents and grandparents were already at the door when I got out of my car. As I got closer, I saw something that I had never seen before, my dad was crying. Seeing my dad crying made me burst into tears as well. I expected my mom to come up to me, but instead, my dad came up to me and hugged me. Without any words spoken, the way our entire family communicated was changed. No more would we wonder whether or not anyone else in our family knew how we felt about them.

Chapter 2

The next day my sister and my other brother showed up. Staci came over as soon as she woke up the next day, and Eric drove all night from California to be there as soon as he could. What remained of our family was together for the first time in quite a while. Although it was certainly not the best of circumstances, we were happy to be together again.

Before that day, our lives had been progressing in a fairly normal manner. Eric was a Funeral Director and Manager in Paradise, California. Staci was working at a motor home manufacturer in Coburg, Oregon. My Dad worked for the Federal Government and my mom continued to stay home and help take care of her grandkids. My grandparents were retired. I had started working at a toy store as seasonal help and got hired on permanent after the Christmas season.

I was content to just get along at work and live with my parents. I had moved out initially when I was almost eighteen years old, but lacking funds forced me to move back. I didn't have a particularly driven personality at the time, but that was rapidly changing.

Due to Eric's knowledge in the field, he headed up the arrangements for Brad at the Funeral Home. My grandfather and I had a plaque made for Brad's urn. We left the rest of my family to grieve. I had the next ten years to take care of my grieving.

The viewing had been set for two days later and the memorial service for the next week. At the viewing was the first time I was able to see him. The whole family went in at the same time. Brad was an avid hunter and loved the outdoors, so he was dressed in his camo for the viewing and for his cremation. I wanted to say goodbye in my own way, so I made the decision to touch his arm and tell him how much I loved him and would miss him. The usual warmth and feeling of the human body had left him and it was replaced by the cold chill and emptiness of the morgue. I put my hand on his arm and felt the body wrap that covered the area where he was shot in his arm, it made a crackling sound that just about made me sick. Although there was no life in my brother's body, his spirit was with us all.

* * *

The next week was a blur of family, friends, press, and emotional roller coasters. Everything took on a meaning and importance that far outweighed anything that had come before it. Every time I looked at my family, I wondered if it was the last time I would see them alive. That was a thought that stays with me, even today.

After Brad was cremated, we filled an arrow with his ashes. My grandfather, my dad, my brother and I went out to the place where he got his first deer. We had to walk for what felt like five miles before we got there. We were at the top of a ridge looking down into the valley where there was a clearing. We all stood there for a while without saying anything. Finally, one of us broke the silence. We all said something about Brad that we remembered. Eric fired the arrow into the clearing where Brad got his deer. We waited for a while, then we all walked silently back to the truck.

* * *

Our next order of business was to proceed with the annual hunting trip the next month. We felt that Brad would have wanted us to go ahead with the trip since hunting was something the family had in common. Mainly, however, we wanted to honor Brad by firing an arrow to the spot where he got his first elk, much like we did previously with the deer. Where we fired that arrow is now a regular stopping point whenever we go back hunting in Eastern Oregon. The corner that it is on is now known to us as Brad's corner. We stop there and have a moment of silence for Brad and say whatever we have to say.

Losing someone that close to you makes you remember all sorts of odd things. Things like smells, sounds, songs, and an abundance of many other things. At this point, even the bad memories were good to me because I was able to remember him. These memories are my foundation.

* * *

The first couple of months after Brad's death I was an emotional wreck. My way of dealing with that pain was to build a wall around myself and block everyone out, with the exception of my family. My relationships with my friends became strained, and eventually, they turned into acquaintances.

In time the pressure of living in the house that Brad did when he died was too much. I moved to Paradise, California to live my other brother, Eric, until my parents moved down there a few months later. I began to rebuild my social well-being the day I arrived at Eric's house. The Gregg of today was well on his way to being formed. I was running away from my past, and I did my best to leave it there.

* * *

I transferred to the Toys R Us in Chico, because Paradise is just outside of the city up in the hills. My boss, Shari, accepted my transfer request from Eugene to Chico. It was at her store that I became acquainted with the local Army recruiters and their families. For the first time, I saw the Army as something other than a wartime hell of a job. It was shown to me that a soldier could actually have a family and be happy. I put it out of my mind and didn't think much about it until about February of 1997.

It was cold, rainy and I had the day off. Perfect time to get on my computer and check out this thing called the internet. I was looking around at historical sites and just seeing what I could learn. I had the TV on, as I usually do while working on the computer, and a commercial for the Army came on. At the end of the commercial, there was a tag on the bottom that had become more and more common, an internet address. I was bored, so I thought 'why not change my life forever?'

I went to the address and poked around a little to get some information. I filled out the information that they were asking for so I could get into the site. Back then, it really wasn't common knowledge to not give out that information. I was already thinking about a job that I could get that would make my family proud. The next day, a recruiter showed up at my door. Since he drove the forty-five minutes from the office to my house I thought I would give him the opportunity to speak.

* * *

He was a little surprised to see a twenty-three-year-old man looking back at him. He was probably even more surprised to find that I was only twenty-three. By that time, I had lost most of the hair on top of my head and was looking well aged from the emotional stress I had been under for the last two years.

The case to join the Army was presented to me over the next hour and a half, complete with videos and shining recommendations from the Sergeant First Class that had come to my house.

As he spoke, I knew that there was one job I did not want to do, and that was infantry. I let him know and he left that entire part of the presentation out. I let him know that I would do a little more research about the Army on my own time and let him know what, if any, decision I had come to regarding service. I was finally looking more into my future for something more permanent.

Every day for the next ten days I did intense research on the internet, and through visits to the recruiter's office, to try and find a job that was suitable to me. The list got narrowed down after taking the ASVAB (Armed Services Vocational Aptitude Battery). When my score came back to the recruiters' office I was called in to review the list of jobs that were available to me.

There were three pages of jobs that I could choose from, but one job, in particular, jumped out at me, 54B Chemical Operations Specialist. I chose this because it sounded like it was a little more dangerous than the other jobs, other than infantry. Somewhere in the back of my head, the search I was doing was for something dangerous. At this point in my life, I didn't really care if I died. I wasn't suicidal, but the preservation of life was not in forefront of my mind.

The ASVAB had been taken, my job had been chosen, and I had all the information that I felt I needed to make an informed choice. I made that choice about April 10th, 1997 on my brother Brad's birthday.

From April 10th until I left for the Army on June 21st, sessions were held for the new recruits to learn little things about the Military, like when to salute, how to march, and so on. I felt like I was being indoctrinated like the movie "1984", by George Orwell.

I got to the MEPS (Military Entrance Processing Station) early on the 21st and was cleared for duty in the military. It was there that I took my first Oath of Service, given to me by Marine Corps Captain Ian Cherry. He was a typical Marine; full of himself and under the assumption that the Marines were the best service. Good for him for being proud of his service.

Myself and one other person left the next day for the US Army Chemical School and the 82nd Chemical Training Battalion in Fort McClellan, Alabama.

Chapter 3

It was June in California when we left, but it was still temperate enough to be wearing jeans and a T-shirt in the morning. I woke up early and checked out of the hotel. I sat and watched the rising sun for the last time as a free man. I took in the smell of the fresh cut grass and the water from the sprinkler system. The sound of cars driving by was faint, but I could make out that they were small gas-powered cars, the last I would hear for a while as the military uses diesel fuel. I saw the car with government plates show up. We got in and we were on our way.

It was a quiet ride to the airport, but a good one. The only thing that was said by the local recruiters was making sure we had everything we needed to get to Atlanta. At the airport, our escort ceased and we were on our own for the next few hours.

* * *

I and the guy who was traveling with me sat next to each other on the plane. We exchanged stories about our families and why we joined the Army. My story was especially funny to him because I basically joined over the internet. In fact, that seems to be an amusing point for people even today.

What was even more amusing to him was the fact that this was the first time I had ever bccn on a commcrcial flight. I was tcrrificd until we landed. Naturally, because of that fact I had never been to any airport except for the one in my hometown. When we landed and got off the plane, I was in awe of the Atlanta airport. I couldn't imagine that an airport would need a subway to get around. My traveling partner served as my guide through the subway and the mess that we had to negotiate.

We had to wait for another four hours before the transport to Fort McClellan came, so we hit the food court and some of the shops. As we walked around we noticed that a lot of other people were going to basic training as well. Some to Fort McClellan, some to Fort Benning, and still more places that we didn't know about. The more time that passed, the more uniforms we saw, the more people with a single small bag of personal clothes, and the more disheartened and scared looks we saw.

Determining why they had scared looks on their faces was not difficult. The United States has been involved in around 250 "actions" since the country came to be in existence. Although war has only been declared by our country five times in our history, six if you include the Revolutionary War, life lost from the actions have been just as devastating. I had never really thought about any of those things or even looked into them at all until *after* I joined the

Army. It was too late to do anything about my service at that point, but I wanted to know what I was getting into. My guess was that some other soldiers-to-be had done the same thing.

The actions that were going on at the time were Panama, Haiti, Somalia, and Bosnia. The US Military also had bases all over the world, including Kuwait, Saudi Arabia, Egypt, and Korea. One thing the recruiter was honest about was the fact that the chances of me having to spend a little time in one of these places were pretty high. That didn't cause any sort of real stress with me at the time, but I was aware of the possible danger of those situations. That gave me something to think about while I was waiting.

* * *

I had not gone outside since arriving in Atlanta so I had no idea what the weather was like. I had a small coat and one other set of clothes in my bag so I thought I was ready for anything. About the time the transport was supposed to show up, those of us who were going to Fort McClellan went outside. The wall of humidity that hit us took us a little by surprise. Five minutes outside and we were soaked. This climate would eventually prove to be one of my biggest hurdles through basic and A.I.T. in Alabama.

The bus ride took about two and half hours from Atlanta, Georgia to Anniston, Alabama, where Fort McClellan was located. Unlike the plane ride, it was so loud with people talking that I could hardly hear myself think.

We were excited about starting our service to our country and just wanted to get going. Some were excited to do service, some for the uniforms, some for the excitement, some for the pay, and some just for the college money. I personally felt like I was serving in honor of my family members who had served, to join an elite group.

* * *

I stayed awake for the ride to the welcome center for new recruits. As we got closer to Fort McClellan, the foliage got denser and I saw fireflies for the first time in my life. It was pretty interesting, but I knew that in time I would have to be walking through this brush, rain or shine.

As we went into Anniston, we went through the part of town that had the dance clubs and some other social gathering places. One thing I noticed was that there were a lot of soldiers in uniform walking around. Presumably, they were on a pass from training. This was a bright spot because it meant there was a chance that we would get a break and get to hang out around town a little.

When we turned to enter the gates, which were unguarded at the time, the driver of the bus announced that we would be at our destination in about five minutes. Those five minutes were the quietest time of the entire trip. We had all seen the movies where the new recruits show up and were herded into military life like cattle, so this is what we were expecting.

To our surprise, it wasn't like that at all. When we pulled up to the welcome center, two of the fourteen Drill Sergeants stayed outside, and the rest went in. We got off the bus and they just pointed the way to where we had to go. We got into the auditorium and they proceeded to brief us about the chain of events that was going to happen over the next few days. It was our in-processing briefing. After the brief, we filled out some paperwork that had to do with our pay, got an advance to pay for basic supplies, and took our second Oath of Service.

We were introduced to the Drill Sergeants that would be in charge of us for the next three days. They, in turn, told us what time wake-up was. Those of us who had facial hair were told that it had to go and what the standards were for hair, which during training is zero facial hair.

The last order of business for the night was our bunk assignments and personal hygiene time. Lights out was at ten, but most of us were already in our bunks asleep by that time to prepare for the next day.

* * *

Wake up was at five thirty am and formation was six am. Our first wake up was slow and the formation was unorganized, to say the least. That problem was quickly remedied, however. We were assigned to one of a dozen "squads" and were told how to space ourselves correctly. With that out of the way, we were told what a cadence was and to start walking on our left foot.

Our first task for the day was breakfast. That was standing in line for fifteen minutes, getting the food and one glass of water or milk then sitting down in a certain order. We were given one minute and thirty seconds to eat what we could. We then got up, put our dishes in the wash area and waited in line outside until our entire squad was finished eating. Unfortunately, this was going to be the way we ate for the next six months.

Each Drill Sergeant took one squad and we departed to begin receiving our Basic Military Issue. For those out of the loop, this consisted of underwear, t-shirts, socks, boots, BDU's (Battle Dress Uniforms), Class A shoes, Class B dress uniform (short sleeve), and one Class A uniform (Long sleeve with coat), Class A overcoat, and our "smartbook" of military knowledge.

This took the entire first day to accomplish because of the number of people who were entering training. We said goodbye to our civilian clothes that we had been in, not to be seen again for a then-undetermined amount of time.

I now looked like I was in the military, I was being paid by the military, and I was housed by the military. The only thing left was to act like I was in the military and be trained for military duty.

* * *

The last two days at the welcome center were spent taking care of the rest of the red tape that we had to endure. This was the last of our paperwork and learning enough basic military decorum to get us into the learning process.

Oddly enough, the picture that is taken to send to our families was taken at the beginning of basic, not the end like you would expect. It made sense, though since we were getting "yearbooks" when we graduated.

We got our TA-50 (Table of Allowances-50) on the last day.

* * *

The next morning we went "down range" to begin training and we all had one last opportunity to call our families and tell them we were OK. It was literally a call that just said, "I'm here, everything is OK, I'll call when I can, I love you." We had Drill Sergeants standing there making sure that is all we said. They had to get everyone through the phone lines as quickly as possible.

We loaded the bus once again, this time a military bus, and we were on our way to training downrange.

Chapter 4

I have had expectations of events in my life that didn't work out quite the way I thought they would. When we pulled up in front of the training battalion and all was quiet, it looked like this was going to be one of those times. There was no one in the company area that we were parked in front of, and no Drill Sergeants in sight anywhere else either. There was an eerie silence on the bus and no one wanted to be the one to break it.

Then the Company Commander of Delta Company, 82nd Chemical Training Battalion came walking out of the company area and got on the bus. He smiled at us and began a short welcome speech for us. Once again, this was not the scene that we had seen in movies when people started their military training. It was very disconcerting.

As he was talking, our Drill Sergeants came walking out and began surrounding the bus. They made two lines into the company area. Perhaps they were there to "herd" us into place again?

The Captain welcomed us one more time, told us to hang tight, then got off the bus. As he walked toward his office, the Senior Drill Sergeant saluted him as they passed and he got a big smile on his face. That seemed pretty friendly to me.

The Drill Sergeants knew that we expected certain scenes to take place when we arrived for training and they didn't want to disappoint us. They had spent the last two hours sitting in the ready room watching "Full Metal Jacket" to psych themselves up for the hurricane of verbal abuse that they were about to deliver to us.

As soon as the Senior Drill Sergeant got on the bus he started yelling and telling us to get off the bus and get into the company area. Once off the bus, all of the other Drill Sergeants joined in. Some of the younger guys and a few of the females were already in tears from the stress of the situation. Most of these kids were seventeen and eighteen years old and had never been away from home. Adults in physical build, but still very much children emotionally. At twenty-three years old, I was able to handle the stress a little better and just take it with a grain of salt.

We were standing in formation in the middle of the company area with the Drill Sergeants spouting orders, picking out people, and making them do pushups. Apparently, this is designed to test stress levels and begin the breaking down process of a soldier before they are built back up into combat-ready soldiers.

Normally, the best thing to do in a situation like this is to lay low and hope you don't do anything stupid to get noticed, like smile or something. Fifteen or twenty minutes into the welcome ritual, I noticed a Drill Sergeant walking back and forth in my general area and not moving around like the others were. Eventually, he turned to where I could see his face and I realized that I had screwed up...nearly seven years earlier.

He walked up to me and I confirmed my horror when I looked at his name tape. I had gone to high school with him, and we weren't exactly friends. I made it a weekly ritual to pick on him because he was perhaps a little unpopular and undersized. This wasn't the case anymore. He got right in my face and asked me if I remembered who he was. Of course, I said I did remember him. He just said, "Good, then you'll understand what's going to happen to you next."

The bright side of what happened is the rest of the company got a break for a while from doing push-ups, sit-ups, and overhead arm claps. The downside was that I had to do them instead. He called the other Drill Sergeants over into a little circle. They all looked up at me and surrounded me. For the next half hour, I was doing everyone's share of exercise. I was pouring sweat and about ready to just fall over from exhaustion when they finally quit. I figured that this was somehow against the rules for them, but I wasn't about to say anything. Just take it and be on my way was my mantra for basic training. I took it without saying a word unless I was asked a question. He came up to me later and quietly said that we were even.

We were ordered to drink water, since it was a hot and humid Alabama day, and said what we always had to say before drinking, "drink water, swoosh!." The two canteens that we had to carry were constantly being filled.

The Senior Drill Sergeant called us to attention, and then he put us in the leaning rest as our platoon assignments were called out. When we heard our platoon assignments called, we got up, gathered our things and went to the specified platoon area. We were to then get back into the leaning rest until everyone's assignment had been called. My first assignment in the Army was 1st Platoon, D Company, 82nd

Chemical Training Battalion, Fort McClellan, Alabama.

* * *

I finally got to meet my Drill Sergeants for the first time. Staff Sergeant J. Franklin, Staff Sergeant C. Alston, and Staff Sergeant E. Humphreys were in charge of my platoon. With the exception of a few people in the company, we were all E-1 Privates. The people with the higher ranks, because of college or re-entry into the military, were split up evenly throughout the platoons.

After the Drill Sergeants introduced themselves, it was our turn. The whole scene reminded me of the scene from "Stripes" where they are all introducing themselves to each other.

For the remainder of the day, we spent time setting up our bunks, lockers, and uniforms to be presentable. Since we really didn't know anything yet, our appearance was the first lesson, whether it was us or our gear.

We assigned hall guard and fire guard for the night then went to sleep to get rested for our first full day of training.

Chapter 5

Everyone was at different physical levels, so on the first day of PT (Physical Training), we took a company-wide PT test. Considering this was the first real exercise I had done since I was in high school, I didn't expect to do very well. Considering I didn't, it's a good thing this was not a record PT test. At the time, I was two-hundred and fifteen pounds. I was five foot ten so according to the military, I was thirty-five pounds overweight. I clearly had a way to go before I was where I needed to be. I maxed the push ups, but was ten short on the sit-ups and ran the two miles in twenty-five minutes rather than the required twelve minutes and thirty seconds for my age group.

With my muscles hurting in ways I had never experienced, I managed to keep up with the formation back to the barracks. We showered and got changed into our BDU's for breakfast.

Standing in line, reading my smartbook, I took notice of the smell that was coming from the chow hall. For the first time, I noticed that all our meals smelled the same no matter what meal it was. The bottom line is that the food did its job and sustained us. I thought I was going to miss my mom's cooking, and I was right.

Once I got in and was getting my food, something happened that made me realize that I looked much older than the rest of the soldiers going through training. Our backs were to the rest of the chow hall and my bald head was exposed to everyone there. The Senior Drill Sergeant, who hadn't actually seen me without a cover yet, came up to me and said, "Soldier, you don't have to stand in line with all these recruits. Go ahead and cut in front of them." I turned around and went into Parade Rest, as you do when addressing a Drill Sergeant, and told him that I did because I was a recruit myself. He couldn't see from his vantage point that I didn't have any rank on my collar and that there was no patch on my shoulder. Both of these are tell-tale signs of a recruit. He asked how old I was and when I told him twenty-three, he couldn't believe it. From then on I was known as "old man" to all the Drills.

* * *

After breakfast, we were assigned our "battle buddies" according to what platoon we were in and where our bunks were. A battle buddy was to be with you at all times when not with the rest of the platoon. I turned into an interpreter for my battle buddy as well. He was from the deepest part of the Bayou, as far as I could tell, and had the accent to go along with it. It took a couple weeks, but we developed a language to be able to communicate that included a lot of hand signals and sounds.

My battle buddy and I constantly tested each other on the basic military knowledge that we were learning in our smartbooks. I credit him and time we spent studying for my later success during AIT.

In the second week of training, the Drill Sergeants appointed Squad Leaders and Platoon Guides to help teach leadership and break people out of their shells. My battle buddy and I were both appointed to be squad leaders due to the knowledge we showed from our books. The duty of the squad leaders was just like a real squad leader. We were responsible for the rest of our squad and were to oversee our squad's duties. Each squad was assigned an area of company area to keep clean and organized. We had a formation three times a day before each chow and the squad leaders would march their squads to the chow hall. Order of chow rotated between platoons and squads daily, and we had to keep track of those changes. Lastly, we did an initial inspection of boots and footlockers before any known inspection by the Drill Sergeants.

For the six weeks of Basic training, these duties changed about once every three days unless the soldiers at those posts did an exceptionally bad job.

* * *

Training at this time of year was hampered by bad weather including lightning storms and a few tornados. This caused a lot of downtimes that had to be made up later.

Unlike most other training units in the Army, the Chemical and Military Police training battalions were OSUT (One Station Unit Training) posts. This meant that we were with the same Drill Sergeants and living conditions all the way through AIT. The good thing about this training method is that when we had downtime because of weather, we were able to do training on our MOS (Military Occupational Specialty) to fill time. It also allowed us the time to make up for any training we missed during AIT, rather than just missing out on the training.

* * *

Rifle training on the M16A2 sounded like it would be exciting and fun, like target shooting out in the woods or something. On the contrary, our training on shooting didn't even start until we had a week-long training on disassembly and care. The first chance I had to even "shoot" the rifle was on a video game in the barracks. We set up a Nintendo that had a game specially designed for the Army with an electronic M16. This was also used for remedial training. The next phase of the training was finally going downrange and shooting at the twenty-five-meter paper targets. Out of forty shots, I got all forty on target. This, of course, captured the attention of the Drill Sergeants and I was called to the tower. I was praised for the achievement, but they told me the odds of me doing that on the regular pop-up targets were not that good. I was told that most soldiers do well on one or the other, but rarely on both. I took this as a challenge from the training cadre.

Later that afternoon we transitioned to the pop-up targets, which ranged from fifty meters to three hundred meters. Taking it as a challenge as well as qualification, I made sure to keep calm. Once again, I got forty out of forty. After the rest of the platoon went through qualification the Drill Sergeants wanted to see if that was a fluke or not. They sent me through the rifle qualification five more times, all with the same result.

* * *

A few days later the Commander called a special formation. After we were called to attention, my battle buddy and I were called to the front of the formation. I was a little worried about this because I had been concentrating so hard on studying and qualification that I was unable to supervise my squad. It was three weeks into basic training and I was about to receive some good news.

The first thing I got was my first military medal, the Army Achievement Medal (AAM). I got that for my shooting ability at the rifle range. The next thing I got was my first promotion, from Private E-1 (PV1) to Private E-2 (PV2) for showing exceptional ability in a leadership role. All in all, I was having a pretty good day. (PV2 Rank pictured below)

* * *

The next milestone for me happened the next week at the first record PT test. As with every other time, I maxed the push-ups, but this time I maxed the sit-ups and the run as well. With this achievement, I earned my Army Physical Fitness Badge. This badge is worn on the PT uniform and shows exceptional physical fitness. (Badge shown here)

Two weeks before our graduation from basic training, those of us who had passed the

PT test received our first pass. It was a six-hour day pass. That meant that we had to stay in uniform and on base. As I was leaving the training brigade area, I noticed that the PX (Post Exchange) was just on the other side of the Brigade Headquarters. I went to the gift shops, bought some stuff for my family and mailed it off.

With that out of the way, I went to use the restroom and encountered something that tested my character and integrity. On the back of the urinal was one of those blue bank bags that businesses use for after-hours deposits. I looked inside to find nearly $40,000 in cash and checks. I put it inside my BDU coat because if I were to be seen carrying this through the PX it would arouse suspicion and I would look guilty no matter what. I would have left it, but I didn't think that anyone else would give it back, given the chance. I walked up to the customer service desk at the PX and asked to talk to the manager. When he came up front I asked if we could go to the back room and talk for a minute. I pulled out the bag and told him that it was sitting on the back of the toilet and that I didn't want a less than honest person to find it. His eyes grew to the size of plates when he opened it up and saw what was inside. He thanked me profusely and asked for my name and unit. I told him my name and what unit I was in, including my Drill Sergeants name. I assumed he just wanted my information in case I needed to tell the story or something later. I thought nothing of it and went on my way. We spent the last of our pass golfing and having pizza.

When signing back in after our pass, the entire company was told to stay in the company area for an accountability formation. Normally, the Commander does not come out for the accountability formation, but he and the Battalion Commander (a Lieutenant Colonel) were both present. This was either incredibly bad or incredibly good news. We were called to attention, and once again, my battle buddy and I were called out.

The Battalion Commander, LTC Robert McNamara, proceeded to tell the company about a phone call he had received earlier that day from the manager of the PX. He told the company the whole story of what happened and said that it was a good example of honor and integrity. While I was golfing, having pizza and goofing off, the Battalion Commander put me in for an award and the Brigade Commander, Colonel Larry Sparks, approved it for immediate presentation. One week after receiving my promotion and my Army Achievement Medal, I received my first Army Commendation Medal (ACM). I was subsequently removed from my squad leader position and given the job of Platoon Guide.

* * *

The last two weeks of basic training were spent making up for the training that we had missed because of weather, and learning how to march for graduation. It was uneventful and I was happy to have it that way. I received another promotion on the last day of basic training to PFC E-3. (Rank pictured here)

Chapter 6

The Army training program for OSUT goes through five phases. The phases are Red, White, Blue, Black, and Gold. Each new phase represents an advancement in military training and allows more freedoms to the soldiers in training. Basic training was Red and White phase rolled into one. Graduation from basic training signaled our move from White phase into Blue phase. More importantly, it signified that we were now eligible for an overnight pass if we were good enough to earn it.

My training company donned our Class A uniforms complete with all decorations earned to that point. We marched the mile and a half to the parade grounds to march for the General to complete commencement. Once in formation with the other classes that were graduating, we unfurled our company colors.

Up until that point, we had not earned the right to fly our colors, so they were tied and rolled up to the staff. The colors for the Chemical Corps are Cobalt Blue and Gold. The flag itself was blue and printed on it was the Gold retorts with the letter "D" on the side because we were "Delta" company, 82nd Training Battalion.

At the end of the ceremony, we were brought to attention, saluted the Commanding General, and were marched off the field and back to the barracks.

* * *

Upon graduation from basic training, the recruits are given an overnight pass if they are in OSUT. Our class was denied the pass simply because of the amount of training that was missed during the red and white phases. Instead, we were given two-day passes from 9 am to 6 pm and we were not allowed off the post. This was not exactly what we were expecting, but any break at this point was a good thing.

Our day passes normally required us to wear either our class A or B uniforms, or our BDU's (Battle Dress Uniforms...Camos), but we were authorized by the Brigade Commander to wear our civilian clothes. After PT and breakfast, we had a 7 am formation to inform us of the decision. We were allowed access to our civilian bags, which had been locked in a locker since basic training began, to change and be back in formation two hours later.

It was almost like Christmas as the locker was unlocked and our bags were given to us. Just to have the opportunity to wear normal clothes was reward enough for graduating, but to be able to intermingle with regular soldiers was an added benefit.

As we were getting dressed we realized something for the first time. Over the last six weeks, we had been going through many changes, both socially and individually. The most obvious of these changes were our body shapes. I myself was over two-hundred pounds when I left for training...I was now down to around one hundred and sixty pounds. That story was repeated with seventy-five percent of the class. The females in training did not have their weight fluctuate as much as the men, so most did not have to contend with clothes that did not fit.

My platoon decided to exchange clothes. If someone had clothes that fit someone else, they traded. We pitched in money for those who were left to buy clothes.

We had our formation and were given the usual safety brief...have fun, be safe, don't do anything stupid, and stay out of trouble. After the formation, all the men in the platoon headed for the PX, which was just on the other side of the Brigade Headquarters. We were like a pack of wolves being set loose on a herd of elk when we went into the store. We loaded up on two days' worth of clothes and snacks and went our separate ways.

* * *

Four of us that had become good friends through training got together and went across the street to the Burger King. Trips to fast food chains while I was growing up were common for me before I joined the Army, so I didn't think anything of stopping and having it this time. I had already seen the outward physical effects that basic training had on me, now I was about to see the inner physiological effects. I had gone so long without junk food that my body had learned to survive without it, and as a consequence, it was also wanting to reject it. Within ten minutes of finishing what I ordered, I was suffering from a massive stomach ache and a pounding headache. A lesson was learned.

Up to this point, I had only spent six hours in 'freedom' since I arrived at Fort McClellan, Alabama. I decided to spend the next six hours seeing what the base had to offer. The first of these offerings was a go cart racing track about a block from the Burger King. It was perfect for a four-person group because there were four cars on the track at one time. After about an hour of back to back races, it was made apparent that we should stop driving in circles and that car sickness can attack at any time. Details omitted, we decided to see what else was on the base.

Lined up outside the PX was a line of taxi cabs for the recruits on a pass to rent for the day. Since none of us had cars, it was our only way to get around. Besides, they probably knew the base better than we did. We climbed aboard and were on our way.

* * *

Given that it was Saturday, it was hard for us to imagine anything that might be happening on base. After all, it was a weekend. As we had the cab driver drive around the base, we noticed a disturbing trend in the motor pools we were passing. Not only were people working in nearly all of them, but they also seemed to be packing up all the equipment.

We found out from the driver that Fort McClellan was put on a military chopping block because President Clinton was closing bases to save "unnecessary military spending." We were seeing the first phase of the base shutting down from the full-time military occupation. The last class to roll through Fort McClellan was going to arrive shortly before my class graduated from AIT.

We continued the tour of the base and were able to see the history tied up there. Included was the W.A.C. (Women's Army Corps) museum, the Chemical Corps museum, and the Military Police museum. We knew that we would end up at the Chemical Corps museum during AIT so we decided to forgo it and keep going. Most interesting were the static displays of military vehicles from the past. Everything from artillery to the all the chemical vehicles in use from World War II to the present.

The tour being complete, we decided to spend the last of our time at the bowling alley, just hanging out and getting to know the other people who were there.

* * *

As people returned to the training area, we were put into formation to await the stragglers. After the six o'clock cut off for our pass had gone by, the unfortunate people who came in from then on were put in their own formation in the middle of the four platoons. First and Second platoon faced one way toward the middle of the training area. Third and Fourth platoon were on the other side of the training area facing toward

First and Second Platoon. We could all see everyone else in the company.

Eighteen or so people came back late and one did not come back at all. For those who did come back late, they had a choice to spend an hour doing push-ups and various other exercises or receive a Company Grade Article 15. The Article 15 is the military equivalent of a misdemeanor. The soldiers who get in a little trouble, lose privileges and sometimes rank. It is accompanied by fifteen days of restriction and fifteen days of extra duty. Since most of them had no rank to lose, they figured they would have lost any future privileges and they would have a permanent black mark on their records. They chose the exercise over the Article 15, even though extra duty and restriction were still imposed. We were all restricted and had extra duty anyway, since we were still in training, so they made a wise choice. Tiring as it was, they thought so too.

* * *

The next day when we left for the second half of our pass, the recruits who arrived late coming back the previous day had already started their punishment. The group that I was hanging out with decided to go golfing that day and arrive back an hour early, just to be safe.

Upon arrival at the golf course, we noticed that we would have to wait for a while before we were able to start. Some other soldiers who were there came up to us and said that golfing without beer is a sin. While we all agreed, we told them that it would have to wait until after AIT was over. They simply told us that was a good idea and told us that we could take their place in the tee-off lineup. They seemed oddly surprised that we didn't try to leave post or drink alcohol in a place where we were unlikely to get caught. Once again, we told them that it would have to wait until after AIT.

The soldiers we were talking to happened to be assigned to the Training Brigade Headquarters and knew exactly what we were. They did not have to test, but I guess curiosity was getting the better of them.

* * *

We were gathered into formation as we returned much like the day before, with one exception, no one was late this time. We were told our schedule for the next day and released to our platoon areas for the rest of day. Being released to the platoon area meant barracks maintenance, study time, and uniform prep time.

We were relieved because we needed the prep time. The addition of civilian clothes to our lockers took some time to prepare because they had to be kept in the same condition as our military equipment.

We completed all of our tasks for the night and hit the sack.

Chapter 7

The next day came entirely too early. What preceded my first day of AIT was one of those nights where it seems like all you do is blink and it is time to get up. Tired, sick, and unprepared for what was about to happen was no way to start a career, but I was going to have to deal with it.

We formed up and marched the two miles to the Chemical School. When we got there I expected a welcome similar to the one we got upon arrival to basic training. On the contrary, we were treated with a level of respect that we had not enjoyed to this point. The company was split up by platoon and assigned instructors. We reformed in front of our instructors and entered the schoolhouse.

* * *

My first class was on calculating a downwind message. Basically, this is calculating the fallout pattern of a bomb based on wind direction, wind speed, the size of the bombs, and several other factors. This is where a person really starts to learn the effects of the explosions they see on TV.

I chose the job of Chemical Operations Specialist from the list because it seemed dangerous and exciting. The more I learned about what I was going to be responsible for, the more the job seemed more dangerous and less exciting. This would eventually prove to be true for most of my classes.

* * *

As the week rolled on, the stress of school during the day and extra make-up training at night was beginning to take its toll on some of the people. We knew from our Monday morning briefing that we were going to have a full day and night of training as opposed to the usual half day. The cost of weather delays was going to become even more apparent as AIT wore on.

We had daily tests on the subject matter that we learned the day before. This not only tested us but decided whether or not we were going to be around for any more training. The subjects we were learning, from fallout predictions to radio communications, were no longer just training for us. We had such a large class going in that requirements were either pass or you were out, no second chances. If there were extenuating circumstances, you may be rolled into the next class.

As we formed up for the march back to barracks on Friday, the Drill Sergeants informed us that there would be an announcement after dinner chow. The march back was relatively quiet and unmotivated, except for the cadence being called by the Platoon Guides because we were dreading the announcement. To us, this meant that we were going to have to do more training.

As it turned out, the Company Commander was going to make an announcement about twelve lucky people who would be chosen to receive extra training at night. In this case, the extra training was a good thing. The top three people from each platoon were selected to attend "Chem-star" training at night. I was one of the lucky twelve.

* * *

At breakfast chow the next morning one of the recruits who had been falling behind physically and in school had finally fallen off the edge. He had already been put on suicide watch for his actions and some disturbing things that he had been saying. While the rest of the company was not egging him on and messing with him, we were not exactly helping either. This may have been one of those times when ignoring the person was just not the right thing to do.

While we were waiting in line to enter the chow hall and reading our smartbooks, he let out an exasperated sigh, turned toward the brick wall of the chow hall, running full speed, he rammed his head into the wall.

We had all been in fairly good moods up until that point but seeing that put us all in a little shock. Watching this poor soul lying there on the ground, having a clear thought was next to impossible. It was like watching a slow motion replay that lives with me today. When you see someone die, you do not easily forget that image. I see his skull caving in, I hear the bones cracking as the momentum from his two-hundred and forty-pound body easily snapped his neck, I see the blood on the wall, I see his brain exposed, and I see his lifeless eyes looking at me as if to ask, 'why didn't you help me?' As the Drill Sergeants converged on the scene, we were ordered to go back to the training area and form up.

The entire company was standing in formation for nearly an hour. Finally, the Drill Sergeants, Company Commander, and the Battalion Commander showed up. We were called to attention and the Battalion Commander made the announcement that our fellow soldier had died due to head trauma. Training was canceled for the weekend and we were all ordered to call our family members. A therapist was called to help anyone that may have had issues they needed help with. We took the opportunity to call our families but declined the therapists.

* * *

Another tradition that goes along with finishing basic training and moving into AIT is unfurling the guidon. Going through basic training we have a guidon, but it is wrapped around the pole so it does not fly in the wind. It shows that we are still in basic training and should be treated as such.

The unfurling ceremony happened the next day in the company formation before breakfast. The Brigade Commander was there for the ceremony to perform a specific function. When the guidon was let loose, he called the company to attention and hung our first streamer on the top. It was a black streamer that read "RIP, forever a soldier." It was a tribute and memorial for the soldier who had died the day before. It was a somber, yet great day.

* * *

One major hurdle to graduation from AIT was going through the CDTF (Chemical Defense Training Facility). The point of this facility is to have the soldiers practice the skills they have learned in an actual chemical environment. Soldiers are fitted with brand new MOPP gear (Mission Oriented Protective Posture) and sent into the basement of the facility. The basement is flooded with live nerve agent and the soldiers conduct readings with the equipment they had been learning to use to check for levels of agent as well as looking for what kind of agent it is.

There are several rooms in the facility, each with its own experiment that has to be done. I had made it through all the rooms before I came to the room that I would never forget. I walked through the door and saw a Vietnam-era jeep. I had to take out a chemical testing packet, break open the agent detection pod, then hang it on the wall so it could get a clean detection. All was good until I turned around and went to hang it on the wall. This was when I found out that the sleeves on the top that I was wearing were a little too short for me. When I extended my arm to hang the kit, the sleeve pulled back and exposed about two inches of my arm. I remember feeling a panic come over me as I was turning to face the Drill Sergeant that was in the room with me. The last thing I remember was seeing the DS hit an emergency button to clear the room.

I woke up the next day with a searing pain in my leg from where the DS had injected me with Atropine and 2 Pam Chloride to neutralize the nerve agent. I looked around and saw that I was in the hospital in a recovery room. Around me stood my battle buddy and my Senior Drill Sergeant. The SDS called my Commander as soon as I woke up to let him know that I was OK.

I stayed in the hospital until the next morning and I was taken back to my training unit. I was to give my company a small speech about the effectiveness of the chemical suit and the agent neutralizer that is standard issue for

all soldiers in a combat environment. I got to
see first-hand that my training was effective.

Chapter 8

The rest of AIT was a barrage of make-up days for basic training, chemical school classes, and extra training at the Brigade headquarters. Most people didn't have time to get overly stressed out or have our minds wander too much into the realm of "why did I do this." The extra time we did have was spent doing research on which duty stations we wanted to pick and planning for competitions against the other platoons in Drill & Ceremonies (D & C).

At the time, the most deployed unit in the Army was the 10th Mountain Division in Fort Drum, New York. While this did appeal to me, I did not even consider this duty station because it was in the North East. I asked to be stationed in the South or the West. I wanted to either be warm or close to home so I could see my family. As the Army does, they assigned to me, Fort Drum... figures.

During basic, we had to march everywhere and carry all of our gear. Once we made it to AIT, we were assigned vehicles to drive for our field training. These consisted of Humvees and LMTV's. The Humvees were smoke vehicles and the LMTV's were designated for decon missions. I was given a smoke vehicle and there was just two of us in each smoker. Being a higher rank, I was designated as the vehicle TC (Track Commander) or "Actual." My driver, or "Delta" was an E-1 with limited motivation. Since she did not have her license, she could not operate the smoker so I had to drive, work the radio, and operate the smoker on my own. Her only function was to look out for other vehicles or obstacles in the road to make sure there were no collisions.

The field exercise for AIT was a two-week mission. It was nice to have that time off, but we missed the comfort of the classroom. I guess we kind of got complacent, which is not good in this environment. We loaded up our vehicles and moved out to the field location for our exercise.

The set up for our gear was a lot easier this time. Mainly because we couldn't have anything too permanent except for the TOC (Tactical Operations Center). Everyone else had to be ready to move out for missions at the drop of a hat. During this exercise, we were able to employ all of the skills we had learned through basic and AIT. While we're supposed to be suffering a little bit to learn what combat in a chemical unit would be like, it was also a time for all of us to realize that our training was still somewhere in our heads and that we should be confident with what we were doing.

We went to a different training ground for this FTX as well. We were further South and the area was swampy and bog-like. As we were gearing up for our land navigation portion of the FTX I was given a Beretta 9mm...fully loaded! I found this to be a little odd considering the fact that we should have been using blanks. I was told that if circumstances came to be that I would need to use it, I would know.

As we were going through the course and being careful not to alert our enemies, the reason for the handgun became clear. I was the point man at the time when my entire squad went running by me. I turned around to see a six-foot alligator behind us. It was just walking along the path that we were on. I turned around and unloaded the entire magazine into him. I reloaded and waited for him to move...he didn't. I was saddened that I felt like I had to kill it, but I didn't want to take a chance on getting hurt myself.

At the end of the field exercise, as with all training, we conducted an AAR (After Action Review). We performed our jobs well with only one incident, one person had rear-ended another because they didn't follow the plan. Most smoke missions are static walls of smoke because we are only concealing from one direction. However, when we have a smoke mission where we have to conceal from all sides, like a landing zone for troop deployment, we have to constantly move. The idea is to have a wall of smoke around the entire LZ (Landing Zone) with open air in the middle so troops can be safely deployed. We have to move fast enough so that it is a complete wall, but slow enough that the smoke fills the wall. Roughly fifteen miles per hour, depending on the wind speed. We had one driver only going ten miles per hour, which is what caused the accident. To understand how that happened at a slow speed, you have to know how thick the smoke is that we are putting out of our smokers during a mission. On the back of the smoker are two smoke pods and a five-hundred-gallon tank of fog oil to produce the smoke. With both pods running, the smoke it puts out is thick enough that we cannot see the front of our vehicles. We use landmarks out to the side of the vehicle and extremely accurate GPS signals to guide us. It is rare that we are ever looking forward during a smoke mission. With the review complete, we packed up camp and headed back to the company area to clean up, turn in weapons, and finish our training.

About a month before AIT was over, we formed up for breakfast and the top five soldiers in the Chem Star Program were called to the front of the formation. To my surprise, this included me. The five of us received a promotion for exemplary performance and I received my shield at this point. The rank insignia for Specialist (E-4) in the army is a shield with an eagle on it and it is the same shape as the PFC (E-3) rank turned upside down and filled in. (Rank pictured below)

Achieving the rank of Specialist while still in training is nearly unheard of, so to show the pride from the Drill Sergeants I also got "blood rank" to go with it. This 'pleasant' ordeal consisted of my Commander pinning the rank to my uniform and conveniently forgetting to put the back on the pins. We all saluted and stood at attention while we were acknowledged. We then stayed at attention while all twelve Drill Sergeants, the Senior Drill Sergeant, the First Sergeant, and the Executive Officer all came by and pounded my rank with their fists into my chest. I was bruised, bloody, and hurting but you couldn't smack the smile off my face if you tried.

* * *

The last major obstacle before graduation from AIT was the preparation of our uniforms and getting ready for the graduation ceremony in front of the Base Commander. Through basic training, I had received the Army Service Ribbon, National Defense, Army Commendation Medal, Army Achievement Medal, and the Joint

Service Achievement Medal. This made my uniform look a little better, but it also caused me a little more work. In addition, I had to have rank sewn onto my uniform and unit crests since, when I could, I was working up at the Brigade Headquarters. Full uniform, but I was proud of what I had done.

Chapter 9

Leaving Fort McClellan was a little sad, but I was about to go on two weeks leave and see my family so I got over the sadness pretty quick. The flight home, however, was not so quick. My flight was scheduled to leave out the Birmingham, Alabama airport so I took a cab from the base to the airport. When I got to the airport, the plane that was supposed to be taking me home was having issues. Because of this, we had to fly from Birmingham to Atlanta and fly out of there. This also caused a change in my destination airport so I called my ride and told them they were going to have to drive an extra four hours to another airport to pick me up.

My flight time from Atlanta told me that I was going to have two hours until I left. I decided to walk around the airport and check out the sights until I left. I was having a lot of fun and I made it to my terminal about 10 minutes early for my flight...or so I thought. I was actually fifty minutes late because I forgot about the time change. I got yet another flight, but it was back to the original airport. I called my ride again and caught them about halfway to where my first flight was going to and told them to go back. A fun day was being had by all. I finally got on my flight and got home with no other incidents.

By the time I got to the Sacramento, California airport, I had a bit of a buzz going on. I was in my class A uniform (The green one) for traveling. I stuck out like a sore thumb and because of the events going on in the world at the time, people were feeling pretty patriotic and were wanting to thank me by buying me drinks on the plane. It made the trip go fast, but since

I had not had a drink in months, it hit me pretty hard.

* * *

For the next two weeks, I had to get my things packed up and shipped from California to New York. Easier said than done. I had never dealt with military movers like this before and it was proving to be a pain. It took a week to get everything packed up and shipped off. I kept my uniforms with me but shipped everything else. I spent the second week at home visiting with my family and taking pictures to have with me while I was gone.

I was looking forward to the next chapter in my life, but I had a strange feeling it was going to be tough, but rewarding. I went back down to Sacramento to catch my flight to Syracuse, New York.

I switched flights in Chicago from a nice large plane to a small prop job that seated twelve people. Our pilot looked about fifteen years old and flight attendant looked even younger. Interesting crew. Not exactly the kind of situation that made me comfortable in the middle of December in the North East. With the amount of snow and ice everywhere I would like to have had a crew with more experience.

The first leg of the flight was uneventful, but when I switched to the smaller plane it took on a whole new nightmarish life. It seemed like the young crew hit every pocket of turbulence that was out there and had to do major altitude corrections every time. In one pocket, we dropped about 200 feet. Not a huge deal, but it was very apparent on a plane that size. When we were finally finished flying over Lake Ontario, we began making our approach to Syracuse. As we got closer, I looked out the window and didn't see the airport. I asked the pilot where it was and he told me to look for the little red light. I finally found it in the middle of nothing but snow. He said that was the beginning of the runway and that he was still looking for the approach beacons. NOT TERRIBLY CONFIDENT!! He just said we would have to guess and the floor dropped out from under me as he started his descent. We were landing ok, but there was a pretty good cross wind and I was looking down the runway out the side window as we were going down. Scary, but I couldn't bring myself to look away. Before I knew it, we touched down and survived the flight. A friend of mine picked me up and we started our two-hour drive back to Fort Drum so I could check into the welcome battalion and start my career as a soldier.

Chapter 10

Pulling on the base at Drum was a little odd for me. The wind was so constant that tree limbs grew out of one side of the tree and not the other. I was in New York, but all I had ever seen was New York city, so this looked a lot different. In fact, it looked a lot like home. A lot of trees and a lot of trails to go hiking on. If I closed my eyes I could smell the pine trees and I could imagine I was back in the mountains by my house enjoying the outdoors. Although it was a lot colder.

The Welcome Battalion at Fort Drum was a set of buildings that housed about a hundred soldiers at any given time. The in-processing period took about three full days, at the end of which you reported to your units for duty.

During in-processing, you were assigned to your specific units, issued your gear, oriented with the base, given your new ID, and you were acquainted with the rules that govern that particular base. You were also taught who the base leadership was and tested on your knowledge of the 10th Mountain Division. This was also a time to get your patches sewn on all your uniforms and get them ironed and squared away for duty.

The unit that I was assigned to was the 59th Chemical Company Smoke/Decon unit. Each platoon had 6 smoke vehicles and four support vehicles for supplies. A squad in this unit was either three smoke vehicles or a decon squad.

I went to the 548th Corps Support Battalion to sign in to my unit. As I was signing in, a rather large Staff Sergeant (E-6) showed up at the door and asked if my name was Smith. I told him I was, and the next words out of his mouth were that my things would be on the plane waiting for me. I just said "ok" and went to the Humvee that was waiting for me.

What I didn't know until then was that the platoon that I was assigned to had deployed the day I got to the welcome battalion and I would soon be on my way to Sinai, Egypt. My first deployment and I hadn't even seen my unit yet. I guess they weren't kidding about being the most deployed unit.

I wasn't sure where I was going when I got on the plane, but after about 6 hours I thought it might be a good idea to ask someone. When they told me, Sinai, I couldn't believe it. I asked them, "do you mean Sinai, Egypt?" The soldier I asked just laughed and asked me if I was new to the unit and I told him yes. He smiled and said I would be doing this a lot more and it might be a good idea to get used to it.

As soon as we landed in Cairo we were met by two Blackhawks and were flown to our unit. We landed in our motor pool area and went right to work finding my vehicle and reporting in. The Commander gave me a quick tour and introduced me to the rest of the platoon. They welcomed me and told me I better get my vehicle ready because we had a mission in less than an hour. I did a PMCS (Preventative Maintenance Checks and Services) of the vehicle and topped off the fog oil tank for the mission.

The smokers were notorious for getting fuel clogs and shutting down when exposed to a lot of dirt. Being in the desert I had a feeling we were going to have our hands full...and we did! Our mission was to blanket the base of a mountain about 5 miles from Mt. Sinai so a photographer could get a picture that looked like a cloudy day. What actually happened was a little different. Because of the downdraft caused by the mountain, the smoke spread at the base and it looked more like someone had picked up the mountain, dropped it, and sent the dust scattering in all directions. One thing to remember when planning a smoke mission is to know the wind conditions where the mission is to take place. The mission wasn't a total failure in my opinion, though; at least I got to see Mt. Sinai!

* * *

When you have never been out of the country it's easy to think little of landmarks, and foreign lands will have less of an impact on your life. Traveling and being deployed, however, gives you a great opportunity to see a lot of those places that would normally be out of your reach. Seeing Mt. Sinai was a great start to a history lesson and it was more real to me after being there in person.

The next sight that I saw were the pyramids. You would have to look under a pretty big rock to find someone who has not at least seen a picture of the pyramids, but I was now seeing them in person. Walking up to them I was in awe of size and history held within them. I got a lump in my throat knowing that someone thousands of years ago were standing in the same spot that I was standing now. I reached out and put my hand on one of the cornerstones. I closed my eyes and imagined what it would have been like to be seeing this stone being laid from an observer's point of view.

They were built to stand the test of time, but I have a feeling the builders weren't thinking about them in the historical point of view that we see them today. I got to touch history.

* * *

We went into Cairo a few days later and got to look around a little while we had the free time. When you haven't actually done research about a culture it is hard to know what to expect, other than the stereotypes that you have in your head. I had the stereotypes firmly in my mind so I was blown away to see how life there actually was. If you were to take the people out of the picture and just look at the structures and businesses that they had, you could almost think that you were in LA or another large American town.

Later in the day, a few other soldiers and I went to a place that provided camel rides to tourists. I had never even seen a camel in real life, so I thought this would be a great idea. After I climbed up the camel I found out something I didn't know about them...they bite! Hard!

While we were in town I thought that I would indulge myself and get a beer. I had the brilliant idea of getting a little buzzed and riding a camel. I didn't realize that one of the soldiers that were with me had a camera and he was taking pictures. So there I am, on a camel...buzzed. I would find out later that we weren't supposed to drink while on any kind of deployment, especially overseas.

My friends got a pretty good kick out that until they got spit on. Then I got a laugh. We were typical tourists for a moment and it was a nice break from the monotony of being a desert soldier. We enjoyed our ride and finally went back to camp to try and get a good night's rest.

* * *

We were sleeping pretty well until about 0200 when we were awakened by the sound of incoming Blackhawks. Seventh Special Forces Group had decided to pay us a little visit and give us some realistic training before we left to go back home. I was barely out of bed from the commotion when a training grenade was thrown into the tent followed quickly by two others and then a flash bang grenade. A group of five SF (Special Forces) soldiers simulated taking out a unit of about 50 soldiers. They did it in about a minute and a half. We learned our lesson to always be on guard; a lesson that would pay off later in my career.

Thirty days later when the deployment was over we boarded a plane for Fort Drum and headed home.

Chapter 11

Once back to Fort Drum I was finally able to see my unit for the first time. It was on the old side of the base that was founded in 1908. As I walked around I could see the history in the buildings that remained. Some looked like they were direct from World War I, while others looked like they were from the 80's and 90's.

The mission of Fort Drum was to be a Light Infantry Division (No armored vehicles); to be prepared to deploy anywhere in the world within 18 hours by Air, Sea, or Land. For this reason, it has its own Air Assault School and its own Airborne School. The Air Assault School is on Fort Drum, while the Airborne School was a dedicated company for the 10th Mountain Division in Fort Campbell, Kentucky.

Three days after I returned to my unit from my first deployment, my Platoon Sergeant asked if anyone wanted to attend Air Assault School. I just wanted to get my stuff in order and get my things out of storage. Instead, my PS somehow thought he saw my hand and called out my name. At that point, I had no choice but to volunteer for the most physically demanding ten days in the military.

I was given a packing list to be followed precisely for my Air Assault training. This list included everything I needed for training and also how it should be packed. If we didn't follow this list to the letter, we were dismissed from training and sent back to our units.

* * *

The first day of training is called "zero-day." As soon as the school started, we were assembled for an inventory of our supplies.

Within five minutes, we lost our first ten soldiers. We started with 250. The first ten were dismissed for having pencils with broken tips or used erasers. Others were dismissed for having their socks folded wrong or TA-50 in the wrong pockets of their Alice packs.

The Air Assault Cadre were going to have at least 25% drop out before the first day ended. With people getting dismissed at this rate it wouldn't be long before they reached that goal.

As soon as the inventory and brutal smoking was complete, we started our first 12-mile run. A run that long would not normally be a big deal in the Army, but we also usually have our PT (Physical Training) uniforms on. This day's run was done in full BDU (Battle Dress Uniform) and running shoes. This would prove to be a brutal test of endurance and perseverance. A test that another 25 soldiers would fail.

When we returned to the school after the run, we assumed that the day would be over.

We were all dog tired and ready for a rest. Unfortunately, the Cadre had something else in mind. They thought that we should give the obstacle course a try. Even with a fully rested body, this would be a tough course to handle. To give an example, the first obstacle to overcome is a wall that is about chest high to an average sized man. I was so tired that it took me three tries to get over it. The rest of the course just got harder.

As if this was not enough, we got smoked between each obstacle as we went along because they didn't want us to be able to rest while we were waiting for the soldiers in front of us to get by the obstacles. We were able to experience the best of the best when it came to exercises; things like push-ups, overhead arm claps, squat trusts, bicycles, and draw bridges.

We had to go through the obstacle course over and over again until the Air Assault Instructors got their sixty drop outs for the class. We were now down to 190 out of 250 on the first day. It was ten at night and we were ready to finally have our break.

The next day we started off at 0500 hours and it was decided that we would start off with a nice little walk; a 25-mile walk with a 70-pound pack on our back and weapons in our hands. It still surprises me how much it wears a person out when they aren't able to swing their arms while they walk.

It took until after dinner chow that night to finish the ruck march and we were so tired that we didn't even want to eat dinner. However, this was another choice that the trainers made for us and we all ate before we went into night training.

The last eight days of training were about learning how to sling load (hooking equipment to the bottom of helicopters) and repelling out of them as well. Our first repelling training was off of a four story tower. We did this so we could learn the basics and develop confidence in our abilities. I had already been a rock climber from before I joined the Army, so I thought it would be funny to freak people out and go off the tower Australian style. This is when you go down face first instead of walking backward down the wall. I took a running start and jumped off the tower. I made it down ok, but I got smoked for an hour for the jump.

We woke up at 0600 on graduation day to prepare, and drill, for the graduation ceremony at noon. Over the past 10 days, 75% of the class had either been dismissed or quit so we were down to only 62 soldiers for the big day. When I got to the stage, my Squad Leader, Platoon Sergeant, and Commander were all there to pin my Assault wings on. Of course, they followed tradition and made them blood wings. They also informed me that I was finally a 'dope on a rope.' Getting your blood wings is a very painful tradition, but I loved every second of it...once again. (Air Assault wings pictured here)

* * *

I got a whole three days to rest after Air Assault school before I was deployed again. This time I had the good fortune of being deployed to Central America; Panama to be specific. This awesome vacation spot for the military came complete with mosquitos that could fly away with you, and many exotic diseases for all to enjoy. In other words, it was thirty days in a humid, hot, and miserable hell. I figured the only thing missing was fire and brimstone.

I got to see the Panama Canal while I was there and it was even more spectacular than I thought it would be. It was kind of cool seeing a cruise ship go through the locks and being easily raised strictly with water pressure. The first week was sightseeing and getting acclimated to the environment. I'm glad I got at least a little time to see this part of the world.

The last three weeks was spent in the jungles and learning how to survive in a land that has more ways to die than most other places that I would ever see. I thought it a little odd that we would be sent there for training since we were a mountain unit, but I guess they really do want well-rounded soldiers.

We were learning how to navigate in an unfamiliar environment using a map, compass, and pace count. If we were off here, we could end up miles away from where we needed to be. Luckily, no one was off more than a couple hundred meters. Considering the distances we were covering, that was pretty good. More confidence building for the unit and for ourselves.

Relative to other training, this was a fairly pedestrian training deployment. We went through the basics of a deployment like digging fox holes, securing the perimeter, continuous improvement of our fighting area, communications, and daily patrols. We finished our training and went on back to the base to catch our flight home.

A gift that I received from going to Panama was a lifelong fear of snakes and spiders. When I started out, I was already not fond of them, but my trip there made it even worse. First of all, the spiders down there were not your typical house spiders. They were large enough that if they were to jump on you, you could actually feel them land. That alone was enough to spark a fear, but they also liked to hide underneath the large leafed plants that are all around. I found that out as I was walking through the jungle area and pushing bushes aside as I moved. I would feel that a leaf would be heavier than normal. The next thing I would see was a spider the size of my fist dropping to the ground.

Incidentally, that is also when I found out that they can jump. I've had a crippling fear of spiders ever since.

Now the snakes are another story. They were usually easier to spot because of their enormous size. Those really didn't bother me so much. They were still frightening, but I was able to avoid them for the most part. There were also several species of venomous snakes that liked to hide in trees. I would be walking along and then I would encounter one tracking me as I walked past the trees.

I ended up so paranoid and scared of the wildlife that at times I would forget about the mission at hand. At points, those missions would take me across bodies of water that I had to wade through, sometimes up to my neck. That was bad enough, but there were snakes in the water as well. Swimming venomous snakes and I don't mix! Now I see the smallest snakes and freak out. I even have a hard time walking around areas that even look like a snake may be there.

* * *

At least this time when I arrived back at Fort Drum I had a little bit longer to enjoy myself. I got a whole two weeks before the next event took me away. This time, much like Air Assault school, I was voluntold to report to Fort Benning to attend Airborne training. I was looking at three weeks of something that I had been doing my best to avoid for all my life...heights. At least through Air Assault training, the heights I was forced to endure were somewhat controlled. Not like the freefalling I was going to go through during Airborne school.

Two days later I was in Fort Benning on my first day of jump school. Airborne soldiers have a nickname; they're called 'five jump chumps.' When going through school, you have to complete five static line jumps in order to earn your jump wings, hence the nickname.

Compared to Air Assault school, Airborne was going to be a breeze, at least physically. The total time at Airborne school is three weeks. We have a little over a week and a half in ground school and we spend the last week and a half in the air and on the ground in classrooms.

The mind-numbing classwork started right off the bat. The hardest part, really, was just staying awake. It was going to always be that way through the class unless we were actually in the air. I made it through the classroom part of the training fairly well because I wasn't looking forward to jumping out of a plane at 3-5000 feet. The fact that they were static line jumps didn't make any difference to me.

My first jump was terrifying to me. I had never even considered the idea of ever going skydiving. Now, not only was I skydiving, but I was counting on other people to make sure my equipment was working correctly. The parachute had to be packed just right and the static hook had to be placed correctly. On top of those little details, the straps, hooks, and outer rigging had to be checked on confirmed too.

We climbed onto the C-130 that was going to take us up and had our seats. The whole way up I couldn't stop myself from thinking about everything that could go wrong and how I was helpless to do anything about it. The higher we got, the more knots I felt in my stomach. As we approached the jump zone, a bright red light illuminated in the back signaling us that we had to prepare to jump. On orders from the jumpmaster, we stood up, checked each other's gear, then hooked up to the static line. We called out that we were good to go and the ramp in the back of the plane opened up filling the back of the plane with light...but no land in sight.

The light turned green and we began to file out the back. The movement out of the back was in slow motion. I could feel every heartbeat and my feet felt like they were encased in cement. As I went over the ramp and began to fall, I looked at the propellers and it seemed like

I could see each individual blade turning. I watched my chute come out of the pack and open up. The sudden jolt of the canopy catching the wind caught me by surprise, but I was happy to feel it because it meant that my chute had opened.

The fall to Earth didn't really take that long, but it seemed to take forever. I couldn't control the chute that much because they are designed to fall without assistance so the soldiers can hold equipment and release it without having to spend too much time wrapped up in the chute. I hit the ground, did my PLF (Proper Landing Fall) and I had finally completed my first jump. Only four to go.

Since repetition of training helps to ensure that it will take over in times of crisis, the next four jumps were almost exactly the same. We jumped into different landing zones, but that was really the only difference that we encountered. There were no issues at all the rest of Airborne school. Graduation day arrived and I stood in formation with the rest of my training unit to receive my wings. My Brigade Commander was on hand to pin them onto my uniform. (Airborne wings pictured below)

Chapter 12

Upon returning to my unit, I was scheduled to attend PLDC (Primary Leadership Development Course). The was the class that Specialists, Corporals, and newly pinned Sergeants had to go through to obtain the rank of Sergeant (E-5). For this class, at least, I had a while to prepare myself and study for what I was going to be tested on. About a month in total.

During the month before PLDC started, I finally got my housing assignment in Gouverneur, New York. A small town about a thirty-mile drive from Fort Drum. I would live there every other month for the remainder of my time at Fort Drum because of my QRF (Quick Reaction Force) schedule.

We had some good news during that month as well, new Humvees. We got a call that we were to go down and unload our vehicles from the railhead. These vehicles were so new that they only had between 3 and 12 miles on them. As far as Humvees go, these were top of the line. The first of the especially helpful features was CTIF (Central Tire Inflation System). This system allowed the driver to inflate or deflate the tires from inside the cab per terrain conditions. Lower inflation for snow and mud and a higher inflation for street and gravel driving.

The next system was the gun system that was mounted on top of the cab with an interior trigger to the guns which were on top. Our helmets aimed the weapon system much like the guns on an Apache attack helicopter. The visors contained within the helmets had an aiming reticle to show us where the gun was being aimed. To make it especially helpful, the control of the gun could be changed from passenger to driver if needed.

The last thing was that we got new smokers on the back. We still used fog oil to produce the smoke, but now they were powered by turbines and jet fuel instead of internal combustion and diesel fuel. When we started them up for the first time, we had all 24 of them start at the same time. It sounded like a bunch of jets at an airport. The MP's (Military Police) motor pool was right behind ours and they came running out to see what was going on. When our Commander saw them running out, he had us engage all of our smokers to full effect. They put out four times the amount of our old smokers so the smoke cloud completely engulfed their entire motor pool. Funny, to say the least.

* * *

The time to report to PLDC finally came. The one good part was that at least it was right there on Old Post Fort Drum, only a few blocks from my unit. We were immediately put on restrictions to isolate us from the rest of the base. The idea was to put us into a basic training like environment so we could relate to our newer soldiers that would be coming into our units after we were put into a leadership role. We had our own chow hall, barracks, armory, and classrooms. In other words, we were self-sufficient within our unit so we had no reason to have to contact anyone outside the training unit. While there were phones available, we were not allowed to call anyone for the month that we were there.

The training itself consisted of Drill & Ceremonies, UCMJ (Uniform Code of Military Justice), AR's and TM's (Army Regulations and Technical Manuals accordingly), and tactical leadership training. Essentially, we were learning to be squad leaders within a platoon, normally held by someone with the rank of Sergeant (E-5).

The training was once again, not physically demanding; however, it was heavy on D & C and history. Learning the roots of the traditions and procedures of the Army was important to understanding why we did things the way we did. Among the history of the Army, was the meaning of the American Flag and how we honor it. The Army Regulation for the treatment of the American Flag is, in itself, over three hundred pages long. There is not a single thing that could happen to flag, or any situation where the flag is present, that is not covered in the regulations.

In basic training and AIT, D & C was about following orders for most and calling orders for few. Here at PLDC, the D & C was about calling the orders and what they were originally intended for when we first started using the blue book of Drill and Ceremonies. The blue book is actually and Army Field Manual (3-21 or 22-5) written by Baron Friedrich von Steuben in 1779. He successfully wrote a manual to train the Officers and senior NCO's (Non-commissioned Officers) how to move their troops in an organized manner resulting in a well prepared and rested fighting force.

There are a lot of patriotism-inducing stories about what is in the truck (Ball on top of the flagpole) and what is around the flagpole. One story is that buried at the base of the flagpole on any military post is a .38 revolver, a bullet, and a penny. The reason for the revolver is so that if our country is ever overrun we will never be taken without arms. The bullet is so that the revolver will never be without bullets. The penny is so that we will never be broke.

Another story is that there is a bullet, a razor blade, and a match in the truck. Much like the previous story, these items are supposed to be on the flag pole on every military base and used if that post is ever overrun. The razor blade is to cut the stars out of the flag, the match is to burn the flag so it cannot be desecrated, and the bullet is to commit suicide so we will never be taken alive.

While these sound like stories of heroism and the never-say-die attitude of our Soldiers, Airmen, Sailors, and Marines, they just aren't true. The truth is much more mundane. While there are three authorized tops allowed on poles that fly the American Flag, the most common are the round ball for flag poles outdoors. An Eagle was tried, but winds caused the flag to be tangled too easily. The ball eliminated that problem. The purpose of the top is to keep water from entering the hollow poles and they were used on all poles for uniformity. The authorized tops for flags flying the American Flag are the Eagle, a ball, or a spade. Each of these tops has their own meanings. These stories have been allowed to remain on the tongues of our military because they tend to inspire pride and motivation. The only fact about those stories is that (at least in the Army) they are part of the promotion test from E-4 to E-5. The soldiers are aware that they aren't true, but they are required to know the stories so that they would be able to correctly inform their troops of the real story.

Being a history lover, this month of training went really quickly and I actually wished at the time that it could have gone a lot longer. Our last act on the morning of graduation from PLDC was a Division run. The levels of the runs that are designed to inspire Esprit de Corps (a feeling of pride, fellowship, and common loyalty shared by members of groups) are Company runs, done once a week; Battalion runs, usually once every two weeks; Brigade runs, done once a month; and finally, the Division run, done once a quarter. The division run is the entire post and is usually about a ten to fifteen mile run all around post. The Base Commander and his Command Staff start running from the Base Headquarters and follow a route that takes them in front of all the Battalion Headquarters all around post. As they pass, the entire Battalion, who is already formed up, falls in behind the line and continues to run. After all the units are on the run, the Base Commander goes back to the Base Headquarters to the parade field where we all form up.

The Commanding General gave a small speech about pride and motivation. Then he dropped the bomb on us...the 10th Mountain

Division was being tasked with the police keeping operations in Bosnia and Herzegovina. We came to attention when he was finished, then we all ran back to our units.

We got prepared for graduation by checking our uniforms over and over to make sure they were perfect, and getting all of our stuff for the month packed up and loaded onto a truck to be taken back to our units. We marched to the base gym for our graduation and went through the ceremony with Bosnia in the back of our minds. This would be the only promotion I received without getting blood rank. I was now a Sergeant. (Rank pictured here)

Chapter 13

Going back to the 59th Chemical Company, it hit me that I was now a squad leader. I was now on the other side of the command structure of the unit and had the responsibility to go with it. I felt this as soon as I walked into the motor pool on my first day back to the unit.

I had been assigned to serve as the squad leader in a different platoon, but performing the same job. I was the leader of a smoke squad and had the fortune to have five great soldiers serving under me. The first thing we had to do before we started our preparation for Bosnia was do an inventory of the squad's assets so that I could sign for it and take responsibility. We laid out every piece of equipment from our storage shed and from our vehicles on the ground in front of our Humvees. After a few hours of checking each piece of equipment, I signed off that it was all there and had my soldiers sign for their items to get them back. That was my last act before I was officially instated as the squad leader.

Soon after, I sent my squad back to their rooms to pack up the things on the packing list for Bosnia and bring it back to the motor pool. About two hours later they came back and we went through the same process, essentially, that we had gone through earlier for the equipment. We laid out all of our things on the packing list and took an inventory to make sure it was all there. We all had what was on the packing list and a few additional items for recreation while we were overseas. We packed up our bags, put locks on everything and loaded them into the shipping container and I sent them home for the day. We got a four-day weekend because we were the first unit to be deployed five days later.

A unit would normally have a little more time to get things together for deployment, however, we were the only Chemical Company at Fort Drum. We had two platoons supporting First Brigade, and two platoons supporting Second Brigade. Since we had to be ready to support units as soon as they got in the theater (to the area of deployment), we had to deploy with the first unit to leave, which was the Command Unit.

For this deployment, we didn't have to use our own vehicle's because the Army had unit's share vehicles to save money on shipping. These arc callcd 'Pre-po' (Pie-Positioned) vehicles. As soon as we landed, my unit reported to the pre-po lot and checked out our vehicles. Our mechanics did a thorough check of the motor and body while the chemos (Chemical Soldiers) checked out the smoke and decon equipment. We loaded our gear into the vehicles and headed to our base camp.

* * *

We were less than two clicks (1 click = 1,000 meters) out of the pre-po lot when we encountered our first resistance to us being there. We were driving through a wooded area and some unknown entity started taking shots at us. It was pretty apparent we were in harm's way and had better be ready to defend ourselves in a hurry. Our weapons were loaded, but we were caught by surprise because the intelligence report of the area said that it was all clear. This would be the last time we would make the mistake of trusting "Intelligence" reports anymore. We returned fire into the woods and the shooting stopped.

We moved the rest of the way to our base camp with a little more caution and were able to make it without incident. Right outside the gate, however, we found it a little odd that we had a Bosnian guard guiding our vehicles for the last hundred meters to the gate. We were told that there was a minefield surrounding the bulk of our camp.

To describe the camp, it would be helpful if you had ever seen the show MASH on TV. It was a lot like that, except that we had stick built buildings rather than tents. Every building housed six soldiers and came with a heater and an air conditioner. When we arrived it was about 38 degrees and chilling to the bone. The first thing we did was turn on the heater and warm up our living quarters.

* * *

Even though we were in a 'police action,' it was still proving to be a combat action; complete with land mines, IED's, and engagements by the enemy. Being a chemical unit, most of the time we were secured by infantry units and other combat related units. The Combat Engineers who were working with us not only pulled security during our smoke operations, but they also cleared land mines from our smoke routes when necessary.

The first thing they told us when we were learning about mine fields was, "if you come up on a sign, and you have to walk around it to read it and it says 'danger, minefield'...then congratulations, you just successfully negotiated a minefield." It was a good opening to relax us before moving on to identifying mines and defusing them when necessary. We were taught how to deal with larger munitions like missiles, but mines were rather foreign to us. We paid close attention to the training, but we hoped we wouldn't have to deal with it.

On day three of our deployment, we got our first smoke mission. It was not an ideal day or conditions to have a smoke mission because of the weather. A sunny day, with low humidity, high heat, and a light breeze are the perfect conditions. Today was exactly the opposite. This meant that we were going to have to do a moving smoke line rather than a static line. These conditions are more dangerous because we are moving and we use twice as much fog oil because the wind doesn't carry it away. We used our alternate plan and went out to conduct our mission.

One thing any planner knows is that a foolproof plan is not fool proof. The engineers went out and cleared our smoke route of mines. The route was a circular route that was designed to cast a wall of smoke around a target building so that our Special Forces could go in and extract a target.

A few rounds of the route went off without a hitch. The smoke was hanging around, but it was thin enough that I could see the smoker (Smoke equipped Humvee) in front of me. As a squad leader, I was in the first vehicle in my squad, as were the other squad leaders.

The mines that were cleared were anti-tank mines, designed to let lighter vehicles drive over them, but destroy a thirty-ton tank. The problem with these particular mines is that the fuse and detonator have a cumulative effect. It is kind of like a hammer and nail. A tank would be a large hammer that strikes the nail hard and drives it in with one hit. A Humvee would be a small hammer hitting the same nail several times. It takes a lot longer, but eventually, the nail would be driven in.

The two soldiers in the Humvee in front of me were going to be the hammer that finished off the nail. A number of explosives that were packed into the mine destroyed our soldiers and their Humvee in a flash. Even through the smoke, I was able to see the pieces of the vehicle come apart...including the soldiers inside. I couldn't just stop my vehicle because the vehicle behind me could hit me. We had to act fast and call in an 'all stop.' This is an emergency procedure for an incident just like this where the call comes through and we stop in place with smokers still going. It makes for a less effective smoke cover, but it saves other soldiers from enduring the same fate. I got on the radio and called out, "All stop, condition red! All stop, condition red! All stop, condition red! IN 3...2...1!" The countdown ensures that we all stop at the same time.

With the ground level smoke clearing out slightly, our Commander could see who was missing. The engineers made a path to the destroyed Humvee and we carried out the last ten minutes of our mission in static. We spent the next two hours making our way out of the unmarked minefield we were in the middle of, to finally get to safety. The engineers cleaned up the Humvee and recovered the bodies of our two chcmos.

We all wanted some sort of revenge for what happened, but there was no one left to pay for what happened. The mine field was a Bosnian war relic left over from three years earlier. The Special Forces unit that we were providing smoke cover for heard about what had happened. Their entire unit came to the memorial service and all said the best way to honor our fallen was to carry on the mission and never forget them. One of their squads escorted the casket back to the United States and informed their families how much they helped them out. We were only on a 45-day deployment for basic support, but it was much more than that for us now. They were the second and third deaths that I had witnessed in the military so far, and it would regretfully not be the last.

We only had two deaths on this deployment, but it was two deaths that should not have happened. We did just as the two Staff Sergeants from the Special Forces unit had suggested and honored them by carrying on with the mission and never forgetting.

It was a hard deployment because of the weather and a never ending chance of death or injury from enemy soldiers and mines. Driving around town we noticed more and more how many people were missing limbs or who were maimed by leftover explosives. They had been living with this long enough that they were starting to learn where they all were and knew to avoid them. We were still learning that hard lesson.

People have different triggers that make certain situations seem real to them. My triggers are visuals, sounds, and smells. One of our missions called us to have to go into Sarajevo, the site of the 1984 Olympics. I remembered watching those Olympics when I was a kid, so the last time I saw Sarajevo, it was in those conditions. When we pulled into town, I saw the Olympic rings on the side of a bombed-out building. A little further up the road, I saw the old bobsled course. It was still there, covered in graffiti and missing sections of the course here and there. It was disheartening to know that something like this could happen to a place that once hosted the Olympic games. If it could happen there, it could happen anywhere.

We conducted the remainder of our mission with weapons at the ready and we were prepared to defend ourselves at all times. We finished our time, turned in the Pre-po vehicles, packed our things into the shipping container, and boarded the plane for home.

Chapter 14

We were back home and arrived at a greeting from families and loved ones that we didn't expect. If there was a celebration that was close to what a rock star would get, this was it. We were involved in the first combat actions for the 10th Mountain Division since Somalia in 1993. We were called to the Brigade Headquarters the next day to receive our combat patches for our actions in Bosnia. The Army wears their Division Patches on their left shoulder and combat patches on the right. This patch changes depending on where you are stationed. The Combat patch is received for combat deployments and it is the patch of the unit you are in when deployed to a combat theater. I had earned my 10th Mountain Combat patch. (Pictured here)

This was a point of pride for us because not everyone in the Army would get a combat patch. It was and still is, a patch that earns respect for soldiers. We wore it *with* honor and *in* honor of our fallen.

* * *

A point of necessity after we came back home and settled back into our unit was to go through our equipment, clean and inventory it, making sure that we had everything and replacing anything needed. It was at this time that I would suffer my first major injury while in the Army.

After the inventory was complete, we got everything put away but I had to rearrange my trailer so everything would fit correctly. Since we were a dual-purpose unit, all of the smoke vehicles had trailers that we used to haul our decon equipment in. They usually stayed in the base camp while we went out and conducted smoke missions. I sent my squad home with the exception of my lowest ranking soldier.

A piece of equipment that we carry around in our trailers is a 125 gallon per minute water pump for spraying down vehicles. It was a four-man-lift piece of equipment. Since I only had myself and a soldier, I had to slide it around the trailer by myself.

I had the Private who was working with me sit on the tongue of the trailer so I could climb in and move stuff around without the trailer tipping on me. My mistake was trusting a soldier to sit still long enough for me to do what I had to do. Think of this particular Private as a highly trained and armed kindergartener. I had just moved the pump to the rear side of the axle when I heard an ice cream truck coming through the motor pool. I felt the trailer start to tip back and I wasn't fast enough to get out of the way of the pump as it started to roll out the back.

As the pump rolled over me, I heard two distinct cracks and I lost all feeling in my legs. It didn't take long before I was out cold. When I woke up two days later in hospital, I found that I had three fractured vertebrae in my lower back and a broken rib. I still did not have feeling in my legs, but I was assured that it was only a temporary effect and that I would eventually get back the use of my legs. I was thinking that it would be months or years later, but I started to get feeling back that night and I was moving my legs by the end of the week.

I spent the next two weeks in the hospital going through physical therapy getting ready to go back to my unit. At the end of the two weeks, I was pushed in a wheelchair to the front door where my First Sergeant and my Commander were waiting for me. I couldn't go home because of my physical condition, so they took me to the barracks and gave me a room until I was back to work.

In another two weeks, I returned to work and to my home. Another week after that I was back doing PT and was nearly back to full strength. When my leadership saw how I was progressing they asked me if I wanted to go to some additional training over with the infantry units. I, of course, wanted to get all the training I could so I told them it would be no problem.

* * *

One thing you learn quickly about training in the Army is that once you start going through training and passing, they start sending you to more and more. They reward you with rank, medals, and more training. Once you're on the track to success they make sure you stay on that track. My next training was with an infantry unit to earn my Expert Infantry Badge. (Pictured here)

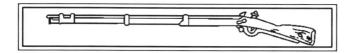

Expert Infantry Badge training was a two-week exercise with an infantry unit to develop infantry leadership knowledge and skills needed to lead an infantry unit. I was already a leader of my own unit, so the leadership part was easy for me. What was difficult was the weapons training that we had to do. We had to know all the weapons in the infantry arsenal and know them well. I devoted all the extra time I had to studying the weapons and making sure that I would be able to pass the tests. At this school, there was no second chance.

I passed every test sent my way without a problem and was ready for the final test of the training. The final test was a twelve-mile ruck march with a full pack to the graduation field. At the end of the ruck march, which we all passed at the same time because we stayed together, we formed up and were given the time to drink water and rest for about 10 minutes. One thing we learned about was that the team is paramount to surviving in a lot of combat situations.

After the rest period was over, we were called up to the front of the formation one by one to receive our award. I was the only non-infantry soldier in that class to earn my rifle badge. So, of course, I got bloody once again. Once again, I loved every second of it. It was especially great for me because a month earlier, I was still in the hospital recovering from a fairly serious back injury.

Chapter 15

Back at my unit, with three different qualification badges on my uniform, I thought I may get a break. That wasn't going to be the case. A chance for Ranger school came up and my leadership decided to take it. They sent me because I was only one of three people in the unit to have the qualifications to go to that school. I was going to be gone from my unit for two months, so I signed everything over to my highest ranking soldier and left for Fort Benning, Georgia.

The beginning phase of Ranger school included the RPFT (Ranger Physical Fitness Test). This was the usual push-ups and sit-ups, but also had an increased run from two miles to five miles, and added chin-ups as well. I had to go through combat water survival and an assessment. There was a night and day land navigation test that started in the dark and ended in the light. Then there was another 3-mile run over uneven terrain that ended up in a mud pit. We had to go through demolitions training on several different kinds of explosives. There was a shortened airborne course. There was a Modern Army Combative's Program. The beginning phase ended with a forced ruck march from Camp Rogers to Camp Darby, which were both within the borders of Fort Benning.

The second phase of the school was called the Mountain phase. As you would expect, this phase involves various kinds of mountain training. Coming from the Mountain Division, I was already expected to know this phase of training well so I was put in charge of my chalk at the beginning of this phase. The first things we learned were some basic mountaineering items like topo map reading and movement planning. Then there was some mobility training, which is how to move around. Unlike normal walking in a town, moving around on mountains is more than just walking. You have to know how your body reacts to uneven terrain and how different elevations affect breathing and how your body changes. This is needed for mountain planning. Planning patrols in a mountainous region is difficult as well, so we had training for that too.

The physical endurance of the candidates was harshly tested during this phase of training. We were given several missions at the most inopportune times to see how we dealt with not only being tired, hungry, and exhausted; but how we lead troops in the same condition. On top of all this, we were in the middle of nowhere with no contact with civilization. For many, this solitude made them fail.

As with any training, the environments that we were in always had their own hardships. In Georgia, it is possible to experience everything from frostbite to heatstroke to poison ivy within a span of a month or less. What makes a lot of other candidates fail is that we were supposed to sustain ourselves. In other words, we are not issued MRE's (Meals Ready to Eat) or go to a chow hall for our meals. For this entire phase, we only have three MRE's to last from beginning to end. Those of us who grew up in the mountains had a little easier time, but it was still brutal. We experience rugged terrain, weather, we were hungry, we were fatigued, we were stressed, and we were pushed to our absolute limits at all times. We learned to be a part of the team and we really learned to trust that team.

The mountaineering training was one of the main focuses of this phase. We learned how to tie knots, belaying, how to anchor, how to pack up ropes, mountain evacuation, and climbing skills from basic to advanced. This also included free climbing.

Mountain combat included planning, movements, ambushes, raids, free climbing, and crossing rivers. By themselves, these tasks can be easily accomplished under normal circumstances, however, we were being tested under extreme duress in a mountainous environment. This increases the difficulty tenfold.

At the end of the phase we carried out an Airborne mission, an Air Assault mission, a ten-mile ruck march, and a planning mission to get to the next phase of training. After the missions were completed, we loaded up and flew to Florida to parachute in for the last phase of training.

The Florida phase of training was the shortest phase of training, but the pace did not let up. We immediately went into an OPFOR (Opposing Forces) situation. We continued to conduct training missions as before, but the realism was increased. This phase began with small boat operations, wildlife identification, and physiological manipulation.

The end of the FTX (Field Training Exercise) was the taking of an island stronghold held by the Ranger School Elite Instructors. The different small units combined to plan a mission to take down the island. We did a multi-point takedown of the facility complete with hostages and interrogations of personnel caught while on patrol. We employed all the training we had been taught up to this point which included diversionary tactics and specialty tactics learned at our home units.

There were only a few who met the graduation requirements and they were ordered to get to know how to survive in the real world again. This may seem like an easy task, but it had turned out to be more difficult than expected.

A lot of soldiers had acquired mental instabilities because of what we had gone through up to that point, which is common under the circumstances. We then had to learn how to deal with those instabilities. Three long days later, we were finally ready for graduation. The black and gold patch was pinned on my shoulder by my Base Commander from Fort Drum. I went back to my unit fifty pounds lighter, but that much happier. (Ranger tab pictured here)

Chapter 16

I was now a Ranger with a chemical MOS (Military Occupational Specialty) so I was looking forward to lots of deployments. That was coming a couple days later when I received orders to report for TDY (Temporary Duty) to the 75th Rangers for deployment to Somalia. Just six years earlier our country had found out in dramatic form that the Somalis did not exactly like us. Now, we were conducting missions in their country that were most likely not winning any more popularity contests.

This was just a two-week mission to perform undisclosed operations. The mission here was not where I had my take away this time, it was the sounds I heard. I wake up nearly twenty years later in the middle of the night and I still hear the sounds I heard while I was there. The first of these sounds is the sound of a bullet bouncing off the interior of a vehicle. It's scary enough to be shot at, but when it's bouncing around the inside of your car it's even worse.

Now, some things a person can do and never give it a second thought, whether it is legal or not; whether it's against their morals or not. We all know that we are trained to defend and kill in the military, and we also know that the moment could come at any time. Hand to hand deaths are a completely different world than with a rifle. We had to go into a secured building and do a retrieval, but there were two guards walking the sides of the building where we were supposed to enter. Another Ranger and I approached the building guards from the sides and came up behind them. Like my first Airborne jump, my first close-in kill was happening in slow motion. I came up behind the guard and grabbed him around the mouth with my left hand and pulled his head to my left.

As I did that, I pushed my bayonet up through his lower jaw straight up into his brain cavity. I could hear the skin pop as the blade pierced his skin, then I felt the resistance as it went through the roof of his mouth, and I heard a pop again as it entered the brain. He sounded as if he was choking because he was...on the metal of my bayonet. I felt the adrenaline tense his body as he realized he was going to die, then he went limp. It didn't upset me as much as I thought...*that* was what upset me, and this wasn't going to be the last time I would have to perform an action like that.

Once inside the building, we encountered several more guards that we had to dispatch before moving on. We were trying to keep our presence a secret for as long as possible, so all of those kills were performed by hand rather than by weapon. All said to the end, I had to kill 14 enemy soldiers before our mission was over. I had to use many different techniques from beginning to end, but my signature kill would be identical to my first kill. I spent the rest of this deployment trying to get the sounds of breaking necks, popping brain cavities, and choking soldiers out of my head. This engagement earned me my Combat Infantry Badge. (Pictured here)

* * *

I was back in my unit after a couple weeks, ready for things to be back to normal. I soon realized that normal for me from this point on would be defined differently. Normal for me was having missions like the one I had just experienced, and not being able to talk about them because they were deemed Classified or Top Secret. This classification also meant that I could not talk to a counselor about what was going on in my head; at least, not until after a twenty-year wait when the mission finally became declassified.

I finally got to have a bit of a break, so I took a couple weeks leave and went to spend some time up in Canada. I had been wanting to go to Montreal since I came to Fort Drum so I went there and stayed with a girl I had met while training Canadian soldiers a few months before on winter survival skills. Like any other time in the Army, it went entirely too fast.

Chapter 17

My next training opportunity was going to be with the medical unit of Fort Drum. I was being sent to receive my EFMB (Expert Field Medical Badge). In essence, this was the medical equivalent of the infantry Expert Infantry Badge. Same length of training, and same ruck march at the end. Instead of going through extensive weapons training, we had to go through field medic training on steroids.

The culmination of the training was the ruck march followed by a demonstration of a dust off mission while we recovered. We all stood up and went to attention at the end of the dust off receive our badges. Proud moment because I was the only non-medic to receive the badge at Fort Drum up until that point. (EFMB Pictured here)

* * *

The army only allows a soldier to wear three qualification badges on the BDU, so I chose to wear my Combat Infantry Badge, Airborne, and Air Assault badges from top to bottom. I was proud of what I had earned for myoolf up to this point, but what I was most proud of was my troops and how the training we went through took over when I had to leave for alternate missions like the many I had been through to this point.

My next call to action was the island of Haiti. This time, I was given the opportunity to choose my own team. I was going to be in charge of a unit of ten soldiers, plus myself. I took my squad from the 59th and five Rangers to conduct our operations. Even though my home squad wasn't tabbed Rangers, they were welcomed and given the same treatment as any other Ranger.

We spent a couple weeks giving my troops a crash course in close combat tactics and operational procedures. When we were finished, we hopped the USS Truman (A Navy Aircraft Carrier) for a ride and were on our way to the island of Haiti.

This was just going to be a quick two-day mission, or so we thought, so we packed light. Our in-one-day-out-the-next mission turned into a seven-day fight to make it out of the country alive. This was normal operations for a Ranger unit, but we had five legs (non-airborne) with us. I was afraid they may get a little panicked, but they rose to the occasion and fought right along with us.

We eventually made it out of there and back to Fort Drum where we belonged. I had the honor of promoting all five of my troops for their actions in Haiti and writing up medal requests for all them as well. They all got their medals and promotions, and I got my CIB second award. (Pictured here)

This was going to be my last deployment at Fort Drum. It was time for me to either re-enlist or start packing for home. I debated it for about a week, then decided to re-enlist. All I had left to do was pass a PT test, turn in all of my equipment, and leave post. I said my Oath as administered by the Commanding General of Fort Drum, signed my papers, then took a month leave to go home and see my family before I reported to Fort Carson, Colorado.

Chapter 18

While at Fort Drum, I earned several medals, went to several trainings with my home unit, and met a lot of soldiers that I still consider friends. I cannot acknowledge all of them by name, but anyone stationed at Fort Drum between December 1997 and June 2000 was, and always will be, my friends. Whether they were 59th Chemical Company, 548th Corps Support Battalion, or any other unit. Thank you.

* * *

I hopped in my car and began to drive from New York to my hometown of Eugene,

Oregon to see my family and friends. As I was leaving post I got a lump in my throat. I was going to miss this place, but most of all I was going to miss the friends that I had made here. My old unit had gone to the motor pool for the day by the time I was leaving, so there was no one around. I drove up and down every road on the base to see it one last time. I knew the chances of me going back to Fort Drum were slim to none. I waved, got a lump in my throat, and got a tear in my eye as I drove through the front gates.

I spent the first hour of my drive just staring out my window in a bit of trance. Once I got to Syracuse I snapped out of it a bit and was able to start enjoying the ride more. It took me four days total to drive across the country and get home. It was the first time I had seen my family in four years, so it was an awesome reunion.

I went on a drive around town and realized for the first time that I had changed. I was no longer the same guy who had left years earlier. I felt like I had taken a jump off the deep end. I didn't look around and see things like I used to see them. When I looked around now, I saw places that snipers could be hiding and ambush points. I decided that driving around town probably wasn't the best idea and stayed at my parent's house for the rest of my time at home.

* * *

I started the two-day drive to Fort Carson and was getting ready mentally to start my new assignment. I was switching from a Light Infantry unit to an Armored Division. I got to choose the base I was stationed at for my re-enlistment, but I didn't have any control over what unit specifically I would be in. If I got the 89th Chemical Company, they were a dual purpose Recon/Decon unit. I did the research for that in case I got to be there.

* * *

Being a person that likes good timing and irony, I was pleasantly welcomed into the state of Colorado. I was 27 years old when I came to Fort Carson, so it was appropriate that a certain song was on the radio. A song by Bob Denver called "Rocky Mountain High" was playing and it described what I was feeling perfect. I was a half hour into the state when I realized that I was home. I was looking forward to the time that I was going to be there.

Before I went to the Fort Carson Welcome Battalion, I took off my Ranger Beret and put on a uniform that didn't have any of my qualifications on it. This worked until about two minutes after I got assigned to a nice, easy Air Defense unit as an NBC NCO. They did my background to cut my permanent orders and saw my training. I was praying that I wouldn't be assigned the one place I didn't want to go. Then I heard it. The Commander asking me why

I wasn't wearing my qualifications and quickly telling me that I was going to be assigned to the 10th Special Forces Group. I had hoped that the next four years would be a little easier than the previous three years, but it looked like that wasn't going to happen.

I was given about a week to acclimate to the new unit before I was sent to the Special Forces Que course. This course is designed to indoctrinate the incoming soldiers into the SF way of life and to see if they can handle the pressures and rigors that go along with the job. Kind of like Ranger school but more condensed, more intense, and more difficult. After I finished the cue course, I went right into training to earn my Special Forces tab.

Most units have some days that are business as usual, but this was no ordinary unit. With this unit, you're either training to be deployed, or you are deployed. We could be standing in formation and told to grab our gear because we were loading to do a drop at a base across the country. We learned quickly to keep our things in deployment ready status and to be prepared to be deployed at any time. We became ultra-prepared to go anywhere at any time for any reason. I had earned my full patch for the Special Forces. (Pictured here)

* * *

About two weeks after returning from SF training, we were at the railyard loading up vehicles for a training deployment to the NTC

(National Training Center) in the Mojave Desert in California. We were a specialized unit, so we had to take our own vehicles to accomplish the missions we are given. While we were loading, we had regular legs helping us out to accomplish the load faster. The vehicles were loaded at one end of the train and driven to the front until the rail car was full, then it was taken away and an empty one was put in its place.

The vehicles were then able to be driven to the front because there were railcar spanners between each car for them to drive across. They weigh about 100 to 150 pounds each. There were two soldiers standing up on the cars who pick them up and handed them down to two soldiers on the ground so they could be carried to the next span and put into place. For safety, we were all wearing our Kevlar helmets. I was thankful for that because I was one of the unfortunate ones on the ground. The soldier above me was handing down the spanner but he was not paying attention. He failed to notice that I had not gotten my hands on the spanner yet and was not ready for him to let it go. It dropped the last six inches and fell flat on the top of my head compressing my neck down and fracturing two vertebrae in my neck.

It wasn't a clean break so not only was I in a lot of pain, but my fear was death from having my neck broken and being paralyzed was at the forefront of my mind. I was strapped down so I couldn't move and my head was stabilized in case I started convulsing. The X-rays showed that I only had fractures, but it was enough to put me on the disabled list and I couldn't attend that particular desert training. Consequently, I spent the next month in a C-Spine.

Chapter 19

I finally healed up and was ready for active duty once again. While I was gone, my Commander had gotten ahold of my qualification records from basic and AIT. He thought it might be a good idea to send me to learn how to be a sniper. I had to agree with him.

I was headed back to Fort Benning, Georgia once again to go through sniper training. Being a sniper is more than just 'one shot, one kill.' We are also trained in the various pieces of sniper equipment, tactics, intelligence, stalking, spotting, putting together a ghillie suit, and of course we had to do it under duress and with punishing physical strain.

Our first priority was to start learning about stalking and tracking. We were all already accomplished marksman; that's how we got to be at the school in the first place. The stalking training was probably my favorite part of the school. We learned how to literally move with the wind. This tactic is for areas with trees or deep grass. The idea is that if you move like the elements around you, it will be much more difficult for the enemy to see you. This was difficult to master, but once I was able to get it down I had no problem stalking the instructors and getting my shots in to graduate.

Normal qualification range starts at 50 meters and goes out to 300 meters to earn your badge. Our range started at 300 meters and went out from there. Instead of using the standard issue M-16 or M-4, we were training on the M-24 and the M-82 sniper systems. The M-24 is essentially a 30-06 with high power precision rounds. The M-82 is a .50 caliber round delivered from a crew served or individually operated weapon. I used the M-24 from 300-500 and the M-82 from 500+ yards. Since the entire school was go, no-go I had no choice but to hit all my shots.

The physical part of training was getting more difficult for me now. I was 28 now and the injuries were starting to take their toll on me. I had passed all of the physical tests, but I was no longer maxing out the score. I earned my sniper tab and requested immediate assignment to my next school while I could still complete the physical part of the course.

* * *

The school I requested was HALO (High Altitude, Low Open) school. Otherwise known as military freefall school. I didn't know for sure, but I suspected that this was going to be the last school I attended in the military.

I had already completed the course prerequisites through other training and combat jumps over the years. I had completed low altitude freefall jumps at night and during the day, as well as jumping from the CH-47 Chinook and various other platforms. I had combat jumps and many training jumps. I was ready to get my final set of wings.

The first jump in HALO school was much like the first jump in Airborne school...except much higher. Instead of going out on a static line from 3,500 feet, we were jumping at 20,000 feet with oxygen and cold weather gear. Our jump platform was a C-17 Globemaster set to carry paratroopers rather than cargo.

I didn't look back at the plane for this jump, however. I looked down as I jumped out so I could get a good look at the scenery. I was above the clouds, so it took a while to be able to see the ground. What I could see didn't look like it was moving because we were so high up. It almost seemed as if I was hanging in midair. I went into the cloud and I felt like I was walking on the clouds in heaven itself. Then I broke through the bottom of the cloud and had a nice shock to my system; the ground was suddenly coming up very fast. I was watching my altimeter and thinking about the fact that we had a failsafe that popped the chute should we become unconscious and not be able to do it ourselves.

In completing my jumps for this school I was doing great and having no problems until the last jump. As I was falling and preparing to pull, I must have been overconfident. I pulled and watched the chute coming out. It worked perfectly except for one little detail; the canopy did not deploy. I had what is called a stringer. Basically, the chords get wrapped around the chute so it cannot fully deploy. I cut away (released the main canopy) and let out the lollypop (reserve chute). I'm pretty sure my heart stopped and I didn't breathe the entire time, but I completed my jumps and earned my HALO wings. (Pictured here)

Chapter 20

I was only to go on one more combat deployment with the 10th Special Forces Group, but I didn't know that yet. I had been given the opportunity to have a full career in the military in four years with more opportunities than most people have in a full twenty-year career. I had received three sets of wings, a black beret (before they issued them to the entire Army, at which point Rangers started receiving tan berets), then a red beret (Airborne), a green beret (Special Forces), my EIB, my CIB, and my EFMB. I was happy and proud of what I had done up to that point.

I was in the 10th Special Forces Group from July of 2000 until August of 2001. At our end of summer PT test, I had failed to complete the run in the allotted time and was a no-go for training. I requested re-assignment to a leg unit. They approved my request and I was sent to C Battery, 44th Air Defense Artillery, 4th Infantry Division as their new NBC NCO. (Patch pictured here)

* * *

On top of normal NBC duties, I was tasked with training the battalion in new tactics for ground operations and patrols, which were going to be transitioning from strict rear detachment to participating in more roles that were more infantry like. We were becoming a more well-rounded Army where all kinds of units could do all kinds of jobs.

My first task was to train them on basic patrols using the equipment at hand. In our case, we were a mechanized unit. This meant that we had Bradley fighting vehicles armed with the usual armament. Instead of TOW missiles, they had Stinger missiles in their place. I had planned a twelve-hour training exercise with the help of 10th Group to play the role of OPFOR (Opposition Forces). My training had been scheduled for September 11th, 2001.

The night of the 10th I had been at home when I started getting side-splitting pains that doubled me over. I couldn't stand and I could barely move at all. I called a friend of mine about nine that night and had him take me to the hospital. After having a catheter put in and spending the entire night in the hospital under observation, they decided to put me on a month leave. I was discharged at six in the morning and my friend took me home immediately.

I got a call from my mom that morning to ask me if I was ok. I thought it was odd that she knew that I had been in the hospital all night, but that wasn't why she was calling. I asked what she meant and she asked me if I had been watching TV. I asked what channel and she just said, "any channel!" I turned on the TV just in time to see the second plane hit the World Trade Center. I said, "I have to go." I called my friend back and told him that we had to go back to work immediately.

We spent about four hours in a traffic jam before I called my Commander to let him know where we were. We were routed to the Community College parking lot where a Blackhawk had been sent to pick us up. We climbed aboard and were flown to our unit. I was still in PT uniform because of the apparatus that I had strapped to me. Since I could I couldn't participate in guard duty, I was given two weeks' worth of MRE's and sent up to the top of Cheyenne Mountain with an M-82 Sniper rifle. My job was to shoot anyone who tried to drive up the mountain without stopping at a certain point and showing their ID.

It felt a little surreal. I was in combat mode and ordered to kill anyone who tried to encroach on my position, but I was about as close to the center of the United States as you could possibly get. I was on the mountain with three other snipers. We took six-hour shifts to cover a 24-hour period for the two weeks we were up there. At the end of that time, I was able to come down and finally put on a regular uniform.

I didn't get my sick leave, but I don't think there was a soldier in the country, including myself, that would want a leave at that time anyway. I went right to work on planning for training and gearing up for war. We started training immediately.

* * *

'When it rains, it pours' is a good way to describe my next few months.   A string of injuries for various reasons had caused me to be on profile (limited duty).   I was able to go out, however, and I did that as often as I could.   I wanted to wind down from everything that was happening and the constant training and preparation that we had to do for deployment.   It was monotonous, but we were well prepared for what we were eventually going to have to do.

* * *

New Year's Eve, 2001 to 2002 turned out to be a great time for me.   I decided to go out that night and hang out with my friends for the new year celebration.   About four drinks into the night I met the woman that was going to change my life forever, and for the better.   We talked until just before midnight when I went out to find my friends and introduce her to them. I didn't see them anywhere so I asked a waitress if she had seen them. She laughed and told me they had left a couple hours earlier. I celebrated the new year with the woman that would eventually be my wife and cringed a little as I asked her if she could give me a ride back to the barracks. She did, and I fell in love fast.

I was happy, so of course, it was time for something bad to happen. A couple weeks after I had met Paula, I got orders to go to Korea for a year. This almost certainly would have put an end to the relationship. However, I had a knee injury that I was dealing with and I was still going through physical therapy at the time. There is a clause saying that a soldier cannot be transferred or deployed while on profile. I took the doctors profile to the orders section and had my orders put on hold for a while. I had to do that a second time as well, but when I went in for the third time they had told me that my orders had been deleted and that I was going to stay with my unit. This was good news because now I got to continue to train my unit and better yet, I got to keep dating Paula.

* * *

Training continued as normal but I was to the point now where I had to take a mouthful of pain medication every morning just to get moving and every night just to go to sleep. I couldn't run hardly at all and there were days where I could barely walk. Even so, I pushed myself for as long as I could and as hard as I could.

In December of 2002, I felt like I had gotten all that I could out of the Army and after talking it over with Paula, I decided to start the paperwork on a medical discharge from the Army a year before my ETS had arrived. The paperwork went through and it was on its way to happening. It had gotten far enough along that a replacement NBC NCO had been assigned to the Air Defense unit that I was in and I had already signed over all of my equipment to him. By February of 2003, I felt like I was basically a civilian again.

Then the whole battalion got orders to deploy for combat operations in Iraq. We were gearing up for the 'Shock and Awe' and Operation Iraqi Freedom. Soon after, my separation orders were canceled and I was re-assigned to a new unit. My home for the remainder of my time in the Army would be C Battery, 3rd Battalion, 29th Field Artillery. My new unit was already deployed and I was to fly out at the end of March and meet up with them in Kuwait City to start preparing them for combat operations as I had done with my earlier unit.

We said goodbye to our families and the last thing I saw as I was riding the bus off post to the airport was Paula, standing next to her mom waving and crying as I left.

* * *

Flying into Kuwait, I had the opportunity to experience something that most people will never get to experience, especially after 9-11. I got to sit in the jump seat in the cockpit of a 747 as it came in for a night landing. We were over the Persian Gulf on our approach and it was pitch black except for Kuwait City. The pilot asked if I wanted to see something cool so I, of course, said yes. He pushed a few buttons and then he and the co-pilot sat back and put their hands on their heads. The plane actually came in for a landing and landed itself. Once it came to a complete stop on the runway, the pilots then took the controls and taxied it to the staging area. I was in Kuwait in a wartime theater of operations.

Chapter 21

We got a few hours of sleep by making beds in the sand until the sun came up, then we started offloading the vehicles from the cargo ship that they were on. They were supposed to be offloaded, geared up, and ready to go by the time we got there, but they had arrived about the same time I did.

The original plan was to drop them off in Turkey and land-ship them to various points around Iraq. Something happened and they were unable to do that so they had to sail out of the Mediterranean, all the way around Africa, then finally to the Persian Gulf and to Kuwait City. A two-week trip for the unfortunate soldiers accompanying the vehicles on the boat.

My unit drivers were there to pick up the vehicles to drive the six hours to the Iraq border where our camp was. It was a little surreal driving through the wire past about a dozen Patriot Missile launchers. The Humvee's were immediately loaded up and we ready to roll out six hours later.

* * *

We rolled out of Camp Freedom in Northern Kuwait headed North to our target of Saddam International Airport in Bagdad, Iraq. As soon as we crossed the border we started to encounter Iraqi soldiers that were putting their hands up and approaching us to give themselves up. Since this was happening by the hundreds, we were not even close to being able to handle them all. We had to tell them to keep marching South and wait for our MP convoys to pick them up.

We kept on rolling North and made our first stop in Nasiriya. Quaint little Iraqi town where only about half the population was trying to kill us. This was actually a nice change from the overseas missions I had been on in the past. None-the-less, as soon as we rolled into town we were in contact with the enemy. Bullets started flying past the Humvee's, but it was sporadic. We found the source of the firing and put an abrupt stop to it by concentrating our fire into a single window. We figured it was just some random resistance left over.

Camp was set for the night and we were on a half and half guard. This means that half the unit was awake and doing patrol while the other half got some sleep. By the time we rolled out the next morning we were all well rested and prepared for the entry into Bagdad.

I was still a little tired from guard duty, so when we started rolling out I took rear guard in the back of the Humvee. We were rolling along pretty good all day and it was exciting to be seeing this beautiful country. No sarcasm intended, it really was historically fascinating to be driving around the 'cradle of civilization.'

Driving North I kept finding myself just staring out the back while sitting in my folding camp chair with my feet up on the tailgate taking in the heat and smells of the desert. I imagined what it was like 2000 years ago between the Tigris and the Euphrates and all over this part of the world. I looked around at the structures that lined hillsides and along the rivers and wondered how long they had been there. If I saw someone and they waved, I waved back. However, I couldn't help but wonder which side of our occupation they were on. Were they happy we were there to oust a dictator or were they military trying to fit in so we could not identify them?

The last ten miles before we reached Bagdad were driven in silence. At the border, we stopped the convoy for a leg stretch and to prepare for the engagement that was almost certainly coming. We reorganized our order to fit about 90 armored vehicles between the

Humvees. They were a combination of M-1 Abrams tanks, M-2 Bradley fighting vehicles, and M-113 Armored troop carriers. All together we had roughly 200 vehicles and 600-700 soldiers ready for our push. I had a picture taken with the arch in the background; it was the last smile I would have for a while.

We loaded back up and started moving. I was fairly relaxed looking at the city until the silence was broken by a mortar landing about 40 feet from my Humvee. All hell broke loose and enemy soldiers started coming out of the woodwork and shooting at us. We were shooting all directions trying to suppress the fire. People starting getting hit, especially in the soft sided Humvees that we had at the time. I started launching grenades from my M-203 at any target I could find on both sides of the road.

High explosives were going off all around and the soft side of my Humvee started showing more and more holes. The light coming through was rapidly reminding me that I was sitting four feet higher than the driver. I was a sitting duck in the back, which was open from the rear, and it didn't really set well with me. In all the chaos one sound came through loud and clear. An RPG (Rocket Propelled Grenade) took out the second vehicle in the convoy, which was an M-1113. The whole convoy came to a stop and the Abram's and Bradley's took up security positions around the convoy.

As we were stopping, the Humvee that I was in took a sharp turn to the side and kept rolling and rear-ended an Abrams that was doing security. I fell over in my chair and looked at my driver. The left side of his head was missing. He had been shot. I hopped out the back and took cover next to the tank.

The Abrams fired a round out of its 120mm gun and my ears immediately started ringing. I spent the rest of that engagement half deaf with ringing ears. Total time spent was about twenty minutes before the AK-47 (Automatic Kalashnikov model 47) fire stopped.

The first major engagement cost our convoy roughly 200 soldiers. Morale didn't drop; on the contrary, we were more motivated than ever to do our jobs. We took care of our KIA's (killed in action) and our wounded and started clearing buildings in the area.

Chapter 22

Clearing buildings was second nature for me because of my experience up until this point. We went out in teams of five and cleared the buildings around the convoy to secure our perimeter and try to stop people from getting killed. We finished after about an hour when a recovery track arrived to load the disabled track onto a HET (Heavy Equipment Transport) and the convoy moved on to the airport.

When we got to the airport and found that it was still held by the Iraqi military. We deployed around the field and took it down by hitting several points at one time. Relatively speaking, it didn't take long to gain control of the airport.

Bagdad fell little bits at a time, but before long we were entrenched in the city and held key points around the town. Driving through the city center knowing that someone could pop out of the crowd at any time to attack you was nerve racking. Walking right up to our moving vehicles, the people were just trying to thank us for being there, but we had to think about security. I was driving with a 9mm escort in my right hand pointed out the window.

We rolled through the middle of Bagdad for a show of force and visibility, with unarmored Humvees and limited security. We were rolling with Army Scouts and Bradley's the rest of the way until we got to the North border of Iraq, at which point we continued our route in a zig-zag path.

* * *

Humvee's blowing up is normally a bad thing, but it can be funny as well. Losing vehicles in a war is expected and even planned for, however, it is usually for a good reason. The four Humvees I went through were lost, not for good reasons, but for entirely unlikely and comical reasons.

The first Humvee I lost was in a minefield. I was out on a scouting mission with my spotter, and I dropped him off at the bottom of a hill and I drove to the top. When I got up there I stopped, got out, walked to the edge of the canyon, and was looking over to see if I could find any blind spots. I heard a click come from my Humvee, which was about fifty meters away, and it started rolling away. I was running as fast as I could to catch up with it, but it was still getting away from me. It rolled onto a flat spot on the road when it hit a mine and made me stop mid-stride. The mine was designed to take out small vehicles, so I lost my ride in spectacular form, along with all of my survival equipment which was in the back. It had rolled into an unmarked minefield. I had a radio on me that was just powerful enough to call for a bombing run. I called for the Air Force to drop a 500-pound bomb on my Humvee to make sure no intelligence could be gathered from it.

The second Humvee I lost was from a roadside IED (Improvised Explosive Device). These are rather tough to detect because of how they are deployed. They are buried in the sand alongside roads any other route that is frequented by their targets, which was usually us. They are also hidden inside animal carcasses and encased in cement. For most people, they would not look out of place because of how well they blend in. We were rolling along just outside of a small town just to the North West of Bagdad when we set off the IED. I was driving by pure luck as I was usually a passenger. The IED went off on the passenger side of the Humvee. The IED was designed to take out medium to heavy equipment, so the Humvee that I was in acted like confetti in a leaf blower. According to the Humvee behind us, it flipped us over a couple times before we finally came to a rest on the driver side of the vehicle. Battered and bruised, all three of us in the vehicle were ok.

The third Humvee was pure stupidity on my part. We were in a town where there was a lot of armor traffic. That is, there were tanks moving around on patrol in place of the Humvees because of the high danger in the area. I had come up to a structure where intelligence had told us a target was hiding. My team and I jumped out and entered the building to find the target...leaving our Humvee in the middle of the road. The problem was that it was right on a corner. An Abrams came around that same corner while we were inside and turned our Humvee into a very expensive pancake. To them, it was a bit of a speedbump so they didn't even stop to see what it may have been. We came out of the building having not found the target (intelligence yet again) and discovered what was left of our ride. Long walk back to camp.

The last Humvee was destroyed after I was lucky enough to find an RPG and decided to fire it. We looked for an appropriate target and found a building just outside of Samarra, Iraq. I parked the Humvee and we walked to make sure the small building was secure. We kept walking past the building because we didn't want to shoot toward the town. About fifty meters past the building a set up my shot. I had forgotten the fact that RPG's kick a little when being fired until I was actually firing it. The RPG flew just over the building and I heard it hit something on the other side. The problem was, the only thing on the other side was my Humvee. I didn't want to walk around the to confirm my fear, but I had to. Sure enough, there was a smoking and burning heap of metal where my Humvee used to be. Seven mile walk back to camp.

* * *

There were many instances during the time I was in Iraq that were fun, and even comical. Even now, when I look back at it, I tell the stories in the funniest way I can think of so the people I'm telling it to don't have to suffer the same memories that I do. I tell the fun parts, but leave out the gory parts. It was pointed out to me that I should tell the gory and let people see and hear the whole story.

By the time I finally made it to Falluja to help out with operations, it was in a lull. A rare time of few combatants and firefights. Of course, there was still fighting, but it was few and far between. As we were rolling around the outskirts of the town, we had kids running up behind the Humvees and reaching in to get anything they could get their hands on. We kept the MRE's in the back and the water well out of their reach just in case. I was having fun watching them trying and failing to get the boxes of MRE's. It had been going pretty good actually, and they were jumping off to the side. I stopped laughing and having fun with it when one kid decided not to jump off to the side. There was a lot of dust in the air so visibility was low. The 67-ton tank that was directly behind my Humvee didn't see the kid that failed to get to the side of the road. Nor did the last eight tanks in our column. The kid, whom I estimated to be about 14 years old, did not make it.

We were finally in a place where we were going to set camp for about a month while supply lines and defenses evened out and stabilized. We went in to the village and told the residents they had two choices, they could either stay there and have our protection for a month or they could leave until we moved out. All but one family decided to leave. The one family that stayed were the owners of the fields around the village so we were happy to have them there. We had Howitzer's positioned around our perimeter along with Abrams tanks for roving security.

While we were there, the kids of the family had gotten to know the guys a little. They would walk around to all the positions and play soccer with the crews that were not on guard duty.

This was much needed R&R (Rest and Relaxation) for the crews and good will toward the Iraqi citizens. In that spirit, we decided to fix the town well so they could have fresh water. From what we gathered, it had been a couple years since the well worked and no one knew how to, or wouldn't, fix it. We got it working again and left the family with five complete and brand-new pumps should it ever happen again.

We also had an abundance of candy when we got there which the kids keyed in on pretty quick. They didn't know what it was, but the bright wrapping of the starburst bags caught their attention. Over the month that we were there, we had been giving the kids and their whole family gifts. One night I was especially tired and slept in the back of the communication Humvee because there was a cot and a personal air conditioner. About four in the morning I felt a small finger tapping on my forehead trying to wake me up. I opened my eyes to see two of the kids standing there with big smiles on their faces. They just said one word, "Starburst!" I laughed a little and just handed them my whole bag that I had sitting next to me. Their father came and found me the next afternoon with an empty two-pound bag. He pointed to the bag and all I could tell him was that I was sorry. He rolled his eyes a little and slapped me on the back. He understood, and so did I, that kids will be kids no matter what country they're from.

Chapter 23

With the fun and genuinely cool aspects of visiting other countries, even during war, were some especially terrifying moments as well. My team was on a walking patrol one day looking for our target when we came upon something that was a little out of place. A tractor driving past a field that needed a combine. We went up to him to question him and see if he knew anything. He got off the tractor and took off running. That seemed a little suspicious so we took off after him. He was going down a fence line then ran over a berm of dirt that was about as high as a small house. When we dropped down on the other side, we saw a bunch of trees and four small one-story buildings. We couldn't see or hear him, but we did hear something that no one should hear unless you know where it's coming from; we heard the sound of several AK-47's chambering rounds. We slid back over the berm for cover. We called in a couple 2,000-pound bombs from the Air Force to come and knock on the doors for us. There was nothing left of the buildings but we got some intel off the tractor that he was driving.

Another moment of terror was the result of a green second lieutenant who insisted that he knew how to operate in combat because of the two weeks of war games he participated in while he was in college. He made the major mistake of not listening to his NCO's because he incorrectly thought he knew more than they did. As a result, he led us down a blind alley with two-story buildings on either side and a dead end. We had to back five vehicles out under fire and get back on our way. When we got back to the camp he had a series of clumsy accidents and was sent to work garbage collection in Balad.

We had one incident where we ended up a little off course. We ended up in Iran, to be exact. A combat engagement was actually the fault of a technical error. We used GPS (Global Positioning Satellite) to navigate around the desert because there were no landmarks to speak of in the middle of nowhere. To load the information into the GPS, we have to use another piece of equipment that stores passwords and challenges, time, and many other pieces of information. When we were entering the information into the GPS, we mistyped the time by one number. This caused our location according to the satellite to be off by nearly a hundred miles. We had about fifteen vehicles and we were getting ready to set camp for the night. It was still light out so we were looking around at the small hills that were around us. The points for our OP (Observation Point) were being decided when we saw something that we shouldn't have seen; the gun of a Chieftain MBT (Main Battle Tank). This would be the Iranian equivalent of our own M-1 Abrams. Soon after, troops started coming over the hill. We all pointed our vehicles to the West and drove as fast as we could across the desert. Humvee versus main battle tank is not what we were looking for. We reloaded our GPS after we were well out of danger and found out that we had strayed into another country.

Combatants, faulty inputs for GPS's, and mines weren't the only dangers we had to endure while in Iraq. We also had a terrible problem with the dog population as well. Unlike the dogs in the United States, the dogs in Iraq are not domesticated. They were essentially wild animals that would just as soon attack us as be our friends. We were on a foot patrol one night when a pack of dogs saw us. They came after us and were hunting us through the streets of a small town. The food was scarce, even for the humans, so we couldn't take any chances and we had to put them down. Sad day for animal lovers, even if dogs weren't the first love.

Even during serious manhunt operations, there can be a little time for something funny. As more time passed in Iraq, the people got used to us being there and were less accommodating to us during home searches. For this reason, we had to find new ways to motivate them to cooperate with us. One house where we knew a target was hiding had to be taken down. We had an M-109 Paladin (Self-propelled armored Howitzer) pull up in front of the house and lower its gun as low as it could go. We surrounded the house and knocked on the door. When the residents opened their doors, the first thing they saw was a huge 155 mm gun pointed straight at them. There was no way we could have fired a round that close to them, but they had no way of knowing that. Our tactics proved to be effective when getting them to cooperate with us.

Najaf was a town that, once again, Intelligence and had either got completely wrong or felt that we didn't need to know about it. We were going to conduct a simple sweep and clear mission so we could check a box and move to the next town. We took two, 10-man teams for the mission figuring that would be enough. As soon as we rolled into the town, we encountered heavy fire and before long were pinned inside a building with no way out. Enemy combatants came out from everywhere to try and take us down.   Our six-hour mission turned into a three-day firefight until we could finally get the word out that we needed assistance.   Once we finally got ahold of our air support, they came in cleared us a path out of town.   Najaf continued to be a thorn in our sides the entire time we were in-country and control went back and forth the entire time as well.

After three days in hell, I made it a point to take a little time and appreciate the scenery around me.   Being in the desert, it made sense that I would look at the sunsets.   Clear blue skies and no buildings or mountains lends itself to beautiful sunsets.   I instantly found this incredibly relaxing, so this became a nighttime ritual for me as often as I could do it.   When the sun was going down or coming up, there were about fifteen minutes where I could look directly at it without it hurting.   As it got lower on the horizon, it seemed to bend to the shape of the earth and smash flat like it was hitting the earth and flattening.   To fight stress and relax, I always went outside to watch the sunset, especially after a particularly hard day.

One of those hard days happened when I went in to Karbala for the first time. Operations were progressing as expected the whole mission until I rounded a corner and saw two soldiers staring at me. Their weapons were at the ready, mine was not. The next sound I heard was their gun firing, quickly followed by the sound of a Kevlar plate shattering on my chest. The force of the impact knocked me on my butt and the knocked the wind out of me. By the time I caught my breath, my team had eliminated the two soldiers responsible. One of a thousand memories that I wish I didn't have.

Ramadi was an interesting time for me. We had been told to not talk to the females because of the possibility of offending the husbands or male family members, so we avoided it at all costs. I was conducting a road block mission when a van came up and stopped. I looked in the back and saw about fifteen to twenty AK-47's. At this particular time, we weren't confiscating weapons so they were allowed to have them, although I didn't know why they would need so many. I went to the door and the woman in the passenger leaned forward and asked me if she could help me. Since my last instructions were not to talk to women, I looked at the male that was driving the car and he nodded to say it was ok. I asked her about the weapons and she was instructed to tell me that they were for fighting off invaders who may try to loot their home. This couple lived just outside of town and owned a lot of lands. I chose to believe them.

Later that afternoon, I was getting closer to the end of my shift. I was continuing to stop cars and do quick checks. I was leaning over to talk to a driver when I heard a click behind me. I turned around to see a young kid, maybe twelve years old, holding an AK and pointing it at me. He had tried to fire the weapon but he had neglected to turn the safety off. I reached out and took the rifle from him and asked him where his dad was. I looked over to the side of the road and saw him standing there. As soon as we made eye contact he took off running. It didn't take long to catch him, but all we did was question him and then we let him go. I thought it would be nice if his kid had a father while growing up.

The crowds around the area were not always happy we were there. So when they started to gather we got a little nervous. They were feeling a bit hostile towards us, so when they started to get closer to me I turned to face them and made sure they could see me load a 40mm grenade into my weapon. They had no idea it was a grenade and that I couldn't fire it that close to my position, but it had a good fear factor. The crowd backed off and dispersed rather quickly.

As I was walking back to the camp after my shift was done at the road block I heard gunfire from the town of Karbala. It was pretty dark and I turned around to see tracers flying all over. We were under the assumption that the town was peaceful so the gunfire was a surprise.

My partner and I took off running toward town and found that there were insurgents fighting their way into positions to try and take us out. We called for re-enforcements and we took care of the situation. The peace was restored after about an hour of fighting. We lost no lives but gained some paranoia.

Chapter 24

One thing that soldiers depend on in stressful times is R & R. The first time I rolled through Balad, there were permanent structures, but they were all abandoned. It was a fairly large airbase, but between our bombing and the Iraqis destroying their equipment when they left, there wasn't much to it. It was a few months later before we got back around to getting there. By that time, the Army had transformed the airbase into a fully functioning base. We used this as a day run R & R base about once a week. There were phone bays, a PX, a pool, and several other recreational activities to do while we were there. We took different soldiers every week so we could all get a turn. This greatly raised the morale of entire units once the runs became a regular routine.

Another R & R base was the main palace complex in Tikrit. For full R & R, troops were sent to either Qatar or Tikrit. The longer R & R leaves were in Qatar while the shorter ones (a week or less) were sent to Tikrit. I sent my troops on the longer leaves so I just took a short one and was sent to Tikrit. The entrance gate to the palace complex was a palace in itself. Complete with artwork and sculptures. There was a manmade lake within the complex where we had water skiing and swimming. If you came there as part of a group, the group had a palace all to themselves. We had fishing if you chose to do that, and all sorts of other recreational activities. The palace my team was in had a pool of its own that was maintained by Army personnel. There were a lot of finishing pieces within the palaces that were, at the very least, gold plated, including the chandeliers. We had a nightclub in one of the main palaces along with another indoor pool. My activity of choice was to rent a four-wheeler and ride around the base. It was hard to imagine that just outside the gate were thousands of people living in what we would consider to be poverty. None-the-less, I enjoyed my down time immensely.

Another experience I got to have while in Tikrit was a sandstorm. I've seen dust blowing in the wind, of course, but never to this extent. We saw a wall of dirt coming toward us and the little bits of sand that were in it were already starting to sandblast our skin. As the wall got closer I thought it would be wise to hide inside a Humvee for a little cover. The dirt was so thick that I couldn't see the front grill guard and the wind was blowing so hard it was rocking the vehicle I was in. I can imagine that if I was standing outside I would not be a happy person. I made it through and from that point on I made sure to always have a plan no matter where I was or what I was doing to get into cover if another storm came along. During the few days that I was there I didn't do a whole lot, and it is someplace that I would love to go back to if things ever calm down.

Back in the real world of war, we headed from Tikrit to Kirkuk. We were following a mountain range in Northern Iraq when we finally came to a break where we could get through. We had reports that there were a few SCUD missile launchers in the area so we were on the lookout for them. As we passed through the break in the mountain, we came upon a field of about a hundred SCUD's and a deserted Republican Guard barracks. Our first priority was to clear the barracks. This took almost 4 hours in itself because it was built to house nearly 200 soldiers. As soon as that task was complete, we began disarming the SCUD's, which were aimed at Kuwait and a few other countries. This would prove to the largest find of my deployment, other than the Ace of Spades (Saddam Hussein).

Mosul was another "fun" destination for me. This was the first place I actually got to put sniper training to use. At the time we were tasked to search the town, it was thick with insurgents that were determined to get us out of there. I was assigned to overwatch duty and found a perch on a roof on the outskirts of town. Unlike other parts of the country, it was not difficult to identify enemy combatants here. They were all carrying weapons and some were even still in military uniforms. My orders were to put a bullet in everyone I saw carrying a weapon. All told, I had to put down dozens of soldiers. While this was one my more distasteful duties, I performed it to the best of my ability. For my actions, I was given the rank of E-6 Staff Sergeant. (Pictured here)

After being involved in about four months of combat operations, I was sent to Samarra East Airfield for permanent duty and operational standby. We conducted daily patrols in the city of Samarra and surrounding areas. We were also tasked with providing security for the many convoys between there and Balad airfield. We had many encounters with the locals at this point. We noticed that there was an abundance of intelligence coming out of Samarra, though we didn't know why at the time. We walked around town with bags full of American money getting all the information we could. While doing this, we gained the trust of community leaders and other townspeople. On one trip into town, we were invited in to eat with the family of a leader. They had tortilla looking pieces of bread that they put their food on like a plate. When I had mine, I assumed to roll it up like a burrito. They laughed and told me that it was supposed to be used like a plate. I just pointed to myself and said, "American," and folded it back up like a giant foot long burrito. They finished that meal off by giving me a shot glass full of tea. I laughed at the small amount until I drank it like a shot. I didn't sleep for two days because of the amount of sweetness in it. We enjoyed our missions into Samarra, but time was winding down on our deployment and we were ready to start transitioning the incoming units to take our place.

One great day I had while in Samarra was my 30th birthday. We had a tradition at the base where we took the soldiers having a birthday and kidnapped them in the middle of the night. We would take them to the water buffalo (water truck) and duct tape them to the spout. We would then water board them for an hour (you know, just for fun). Paula had sent a box full of stuff to me for my birthday with cake and a whole bunch of other goodies. This wouldn't normally be a bad thing, except for the fact that she labeled the outside, "don't open until September 28th." It didn't take long for everyone to figure out that it was my birthday. That night

I made sure that those in my tent could hear my weapon chambering a round. I slept with my rifle all night long. All was well the next day, however, when I shared what she had sent me for my day. They still managed to get me later by catching me off guard and hog tying me to the back of a Humvee and dragging me around the sand at the airfield for about ten minutes.

It didn't happen often, but there were probes into the airfield on occasion. Soldiers would test our security boundaries or there would be a mortar attack. This particular day there was a mortar attack. I jumped up onto an Abrams so I could have a better view of where it was coming from. About the same time, I found where it was coming from, so did the gunner in the tank that I was standing on. I didn't notice that there was anyone in the tank so I wasn't looking out for it. I heard the gun start to rotate, but I didn't have time to react and get out of the way. The barrel of the gun hit me in the middle of the back and knocked me off the tank. I laid on the ground, unable to move, for the entirety of the attack. The crew saw me lying next to the tank when they got out and helped me to the aid station. I was flown to the nearest X-ray in Balad and told that I had four fractured vertebrae in my thoracic spine. I was given a little time to regain my mobility and told that I would be going back home soon.

Chapter 25

I had a lot of time to reflect on my time in Iraq while I was recovering. Several memories came to me when I was laying there; good memories and bad.

One of the memories that came to me was my sleeping conditions while I was overseas. A lot of the time I slept on top of my Humvee because of the camel spiders that liked to gnaw on people while they were sleeping. A camel spider looks like a cross between a regular spider and a scorpion and they were the size of an average man's boot. One day when I rolled into a resupply camp I saw someone I knew and he had a bandage over the side of his face. I asked him what happened and he told me that a camel spider decided to make a meal of him.

Apparently, they use a numbing agent so you can't feel them taking bites out of you. He showed me the inside of his face and there was a hole all the way through his cheek.

One of my more unique places to sleep was on top of an ammo bunker on the Samarra Airfield. The buildings on the airfield were built to withstand sandstorms and high winds, so the wall did not go straight up, they were built at about a 35 to 40-degree angle. That design made it possible to walk up the outside of the building to the top. I chose this spot so that I could have a good vantage point if something were to happen. I set up a cover of camo net for the cot and a sniper point facing out toward the perimeter. We had a USO concert while I was there and it proved to be a good seat for that as well.

Every once in a while, we would make a major change in location. When we did this, we would move at a pretty quick pace and some of the slower vehicles couldn't keep up with us. The Paladin's were one of those vehicles as they could only move at around 25 to 30 miles per hour. On top of that, they would tend to throw their tracks. So we loaded them up on HET's and drove them. I asked if I could man a gun during the movement and they told me to take command of one of the tracks. I jumped in and pulled guard for the convoy with my rifle. Next to me was another soldier manning the .50 cal that was mounted on the track. As we were rolling through one town, the power lines hung at about 16 feet or so. When we stood out of the top of the track, we were at 17 to 18 feet. We didn't know that at first, though. I was looking at the track behind us and they started pointing ahead of us. I looked expecting to see someone attacking us, but what I saw was a power line right about chest high I dropped down just in time to be missed, but the soldier that was manning the 50 didn't see it at all. The power line wrapped around him and the mount for the 50. I tried to cut the line but we were moving too fast. I was standing underneath him inside the compartment when the line tightened and went through him like a knife through a soft stick of butter. I was covered in everything that fell down. I spent the next hour throwing up and trying to clean up. The sound, smell, and feeling of that haunt me every night.

Another event that I frequently revisit is when a convoy I was in got shot at by an RPG. The person firing it missed the first time, so his buddy decided it would be a good idea to help him aim. He proceeded to stand right behind him. An RPG puts out a flame behind it when it is fired, hence the "Rocket" in a rocket-propelled grenade. The guy trying to help aim the RPG was pretty much gone from the waist up. We walked over to check out the scene and I found myself laughing when I stepped on and broke what was left of his face. Laughing!! This should have been a red flag, but I didn't even pay attention to it.

Pulling road block duty sounds like an easy enough job, but even there you can have nightmare inducing experiences. I had several, but one incident in particular sticks out. I was on sniper duty at a roadblock when a suicide bomber came driving at the road block. I took aim at him. The M-82 rifle was designed as an anti-equipment sniper rifle, so it had no problem going through a window. I saw his face and I could tell that he had no intention of stopping. I got a smile on my face, said out loud that I would "see him in hell," then pulled the trigger. His head exploded inside the car and I found myself laughing out loud once again.

Chapter 26

I had changed a lot from the person I was in high school and before. I was far from popular, but I wasn't completely unpopular either. One thing I was all the time, was happy.

I was still happy, for the most part, but I had noticed that my sense of humor had changed dramatically. I don't know if it was a coping mechanism or mental instability, but it was different.

Changes aside, I looked for any way I could to have fun. One way was to volunteer for ice runs. With all the gear we had to wear and the blazing hot temperatures in the desert, it didn't take long to overheat. We went on runs to get ice for the freezers and they would be loaded in the back of a 5-ton. The blocks were about 3 feet long and 6 inches square. I would have them loaded up in the back then I would climb in and just lay on top of them to cool down. By the time we would get back to the base, there would be a Gregg shaped indent in the ice.

I also got amused by how I was able to prepare my food without using the supplied heater. It was so hot that the metal on the Humvee intake was hot enough to heat up my MRE's. I saved the heating elements for later use. Making bombs from the material was relatively easy, so I used them when I ran out of flash-bangs when clearing buildings.

I had mentioned that the only people I knew when I landed in country were the cook and a supply sergeant. These turned out to be good friendships. I always had fresh uniforms and new boots, not to mention some really good food. I came back to the tent that I eventually moved into when I got to Samarra and found an entire pallet of pop inside my tent...which also now had air-conditioning. I went over to the chow hall to say thank you and was invited in to make and have elephant ears. Giant sugar treats that could make the most hardened soldiers day. I found myself having a lot of good meals and getting the best boxes of MRE's to take with me on patrols. I would take the bright spots wherever I could find them.

Back in the small village that we occupied, there was a man who sat outside the wire every day selling pop to the soldiers going in and out. Once we got to know him, we found that if you knew the code word, he also had alcoholic drinks as well. I found myself volunteering to take night watch so I could get the alcohol during the day and drink at night while I watched movies and things like that.

Of the many bright spots while in Iraq, Thanksgiving was actually one of them. The insurgents didn't know our patterns yet, and for the most part, people were still happy that we were there. This was a day that I was able to put aside all of the horrible things I had done in the name of freedom and be thankful for my troops, my family, and the woman waiting for me back home that I would eventually be marrying. The food was great, and for once, I actually felt like things were normal, even if for a little while.

Going back to the company area after Thanksgiving dinner it was dark and we were in blackout conditions. This means that we were ordered to obey noise and light discipline as much as possible. I would have been fine if I would have just worn my NVG's (Night Vision Goggles), however, I felt that I knew the airfield well enough that I would not need them. Turns out, I was wrong. One wouldn't expect something that is nearly a hundred feet long from the tip of one blade to the tip of the other and two stories tall could hide in plain sight, but it did. I was going along pretty quickly, but all of a sudden it came out of the dark. I saw the static electricity coming from the blades as they were spinning. I slammed on the brakes and came to a stop right next to the helicopter. I looked up and the pilot was laughing at me. I just waved and went on my way.

We had to wait for around 62 days after we arrived in-country to get a chance to call our families. Even then, the opportunities were few and far between. We were able to make calls about once every two weeks when we were in Samarra and on occasion when we were in Balad. I had made friends with some Air Force personnel while in Iraq, so when I went to Balad I was able to use their phone bank, which was almost always empty. Meanwhile, the Army bank had a line around the block to get in. If we wanted to call our families during what would be daytime for them, we had to use a satellite phone. It was in the middle of the night for us, but it was well worth it to hear those voices. I remember the first time I was able to call, neither of us said anything for a couple minutes because we were both crying. I had hardened a lot while in Iraq, but Paula was always able to soften me up.

Chapter 27

I've heard a lot of people say that you can't change someone. That they are who they are and it's programmed into them. That's not entirely true, you can change someone, it just takes an extreme event. I had been under enough stress that one day I found out what one of my favorite sounds in the world would be...the sound of MY gun misfiring. I already knew that I liked the sound of a misfiring AK, so it came as no surprise that I would like the other sound as well. I had been arguing with a First Sergeant for a couple weeks about everything. It got to the point that I wished that insurgents would deal with my problem for me. This wasn't going to happen. One day, I had enough and really felt like I was going to kill him. I raised my gun, pulled my trigger, then...nothing. The silence was sweet. He stopped and turned around and just asked me what I would like him to do. I told him to give me a minute and I would take over another team. He agreed and we went our separate ways. No other words were spoken about the incident. As I look back I realize that I have a lot of respect for the man, the rank, and the soldier. That incident shook me up because even years later I can't believe that I would have been capable of that act.

I already had issues with killing people, morally and theologically. I had not been to church or practiced religion at all since my brother had died, but I still believed. Not knowing commandments and passages by heart, I made the same mistake that many other people make. I thought the commandment said, "thou shalt not kill." It was pointed out to me later on by a man named Vic that it said, "thou shalt not murder." This caused me a lot of relief and helped me deal with some of the anger issues I was having.

I did have the opportunity to perform acts of kindness while I was there. One time specifically comes to mind. Of all our enemies throughout the world, there is one group of people who are never considered to be enemies...kids. We spent a lot of time helping kids whenever we could. Helping to rebuild their homes or assisting with irrigation of their families crops. What I like doing the most, however, was going to the schools and handing out supplies to help them learn. We passed out pens, pencils, and paper the most, but we had chances to give them books as well. It was a bright spot in a dark world of hell that helped us cope with what we were having to do.

Anyone who has lived in a climate where it rains a lot knows that depression can take effect quickly and powerfully. That's just dealing with the rain alone. Now imagine what it would be like if every time it rained, everything you were working to build would wash away and you couldn't move. The dirt there was more like baking soda. It was difficult to walk on when it was dry and you stayed on top, but when it rained you sank down four to six inches and it acted more like quicksand at that point. No matter what we tried, we couldn't ease the effects. If we put down rocks, they just sank if it rained. We got to the point that if it rained and we had to get our vehicles out for a mission, we just called Hercules (the M-88 track recovery vehicle) and had it lift us out.

It didn't take long for things that used to be tragic for me to become funny. My team was in a location that was surrounded by and secured by a Field Artillery unit. These guns are able to send a round up to 18 miles to its target. There was a short time when the MP's were using a nearby hanger as an enemy prisoner camp. One night the guns got a mission and started firing about two in the morning. Of course, it woke us all up, but we knew what the deal was. The Iraqi prisoners, on the other hand, thought that we were being shelled. They didn't realize that it was outgoing rather than incoming. There were a couple dozen prisoners and they were trying as hard as they could to get out of there and into some kind of cover. Unfortunately, the stack of six lines of razor wire around them stopped them in their tracks. Some didn't even try while others tried to get through the wire, and failed. They were literally hanging there in the razors cut up and in pain, but alive. I found that both tragic, and hilarious at the same time.

There was an area that I had proven to be adept at while I was deployed, interrogating soldiers and finding out valuable intelligence. I had a real problem with the techniques used to obtain information. In my eyes, it bordered on torture so I found other ways to extract information. I preferred to use fear and intimidation from the threat of violence rather than violence itself. It made me feel a little better about it, but I still didn't like having to do it. To this day, I still regret having to take part in the interrogations.

I may have had issues with interrogation methods, the Iraqis didn't seem to have those same issues. I went in to a village with my team to perform an extraction when we were ambushed and separated. It was as if they knew we were coming. I was surrounded and the Iraqis forcefully invited me to have a conversation with them. Along with beating me and trying to cause me to talk by cutting me up, they put needles in my knees and elbows to cause as much pain as possible. Before they could go any farther, my team had returned to get me and they all died a horribly painful death. As I was being helped out of the building I put a shot in each of their heads as my way of saying good riddance. I hated them then, and I hate them now. Another feeling that I'm sorry I have.

Chapter 28

Right at the end of my time in Iraq, we started conducting more and more missions into Samarra to search for Saddam. Everyone in town seemed to have different intel for us and we had to follow up on every piece of information we were given. Following these leads, we gathered a lot more information and a lot of dead ends. My last search was the same block where Saddam was caught. We had already searched this area several times, but we would only need to search it one last time. Saddam was caught the next day.

The next day I was in a convoy heading down to Balad for the last time. The first priority was to go to the MP's to have my stuff and my things checked for contraband for the flight home. Since this was the first of four checks, it was fairly easy and quick. I had to wait for about four hours for the C-130 to arrive that was going to take me to Kuwait. Once it finally arrived, we all loaded up in the back with our stuff and got ready to take off. We were getting antsy because we just wanted to get out of country and go home. We sat on the runway for about a half hour before we took off. Finally, we heard the engines spin up and we started taking off. We reached about 10,000 feet when the plane took a sudden turn and began a decent, then the pilot announced over an intercom that the President had invoked a stop-loss. We were all dead silent with our spirits completely devastated. Then, right before we touched down, the engines powered up and we started to ascend again. He then made an announcement that since we were already in the air when he got the orders, they didn't apply to us and we were going home. We all cheered.

Arriving back at Camp Wolf in Kuwait, we saw that there had been a major change over the last year. What once was a tent chow hall and tent barracks, was now a small community. They had built a hard-sided chow hall and there were several fast food places that we hadn't seen since we were back in the states. They had even put in an ice cream shop. We were going to be here for about three days, so this was nice to see. We had our things looked at again for contraband, then enjoyed the food and couple concerts before we were boarding a plane back home. This time, we were on a commercial 747 instead of a military plane.

Our first stop was Cyprus. Our plane was cordoned off and we were able to step off, but only to the foot of the ladder while they refueled the plane. The next stop was in Ireland. This time they actually let us go into the terminal and have a seat. This was a nice surprise, even though they had cleared all civilians out of the airport except for one. They had opened up the bar for us so we could have our first beer in a year. We were a little upset that they were limiting us to one, but they gave us 24-ounce glasses and our tolerance was down. So one was all it took for most of us. Once we were able to relax and they switched out the crew and pilot and we were on our way back over the Atlantic to head for home. No more stops until we got to the US.

We flew into Bangor, Maine and once again they let us go into the terminal. I let my troops go ahead of me so they could get off first. I rounded the corner before the terminal to see all of them crowded at the next corner. I asked what was going on and they told me that they didn't think they were supposed to be there. I looked around the corner and saw that the terminal was full of people. I took a closer look and saw that a lot of them were former service members and nearly all of them had flags. They were lined up down both sides of the walk. I just looked at my guys and told them that they were there for us, and to enjoy it. The people had brought cell phones for us to call our families and let them know that we were back home and that we were ok. We spent a couple hours talking to the people and getting to know them. It was a great welcome back to the United States and a scene I will never forget. Next stop, Fort Hood Texas.

We flew into Fort Hood, because of the two hundred or so people on the plane, there were only ten of us from Fort Carson. We assumed that the planners of the flight knew this, but we were about to get a rude awakening. We got bussed from the airfield to a gym on base. We went and stood with the rest of the troops for their welcome home ceremony. I went up to a First Sergeant and asked how we were going to get home. He asked if we were close enough to walk and that's when I realized that he didn't know we were on the plane. I just told him we were 4th ID in Carson, not Hood. They did not have a plan to get us home. We were told that we would have to spend the night and fly out the next day. We were upset that we were going to have to wait another day to see our families, but we understood. They gave us rooms in the barracks while they arranged our flights. They told us that we would have to buy civilian clothes since we were not allowed to fly commercial in our DCU's (Digital Combat Uniforms). This was a point of tension because not only were we not going to get a homecoming in front of our families, but we would not get any acknowledgment at all. Some guys slept, but most of us spent the night talking to our families letting them know the plan and preparing ourselves to be back in their lives.

Chapter 29

When we landed in Colorado Springs, our families were there waiting for us. Paula had planned to have our neighbor hold a banner that she had made unfurled while they waved flags. She didn't know that the plane landed a little early, so I was able to walk up to her without her noticing because her back was to the ramp and she was talking on the phone to her family. I tapped her on the shoulder and when she turned around she had a look of surprise on her face. It took a couple seconds for it all to sink in, but she teared up and gave me a hug and a kiss. She moved back and waved the flags and said, "welcome home!" Then she hugged me again and wouldn't let go. Being a military town, the people recognized the bag on my shoulder and the welcome I got when I got off the plane. I got the best welcome home that I could have asked for, I got Paula.

On arrival back onto post, I was told that I would be wearing the rank of Sergeant First Class because I was going to be in charge of the rear detachment and the companies would be reporting to me until a First Sergeant came home a month later. (Rank pictured here)

We went through another contraband inspection and then everyone disappeared. We were to report daily in the morning and then at five for the end of the day accountability and retreat. For many of us, we were starting to work our way back into civilian life and getting ready to move on. For others, they were transitioning to other duty stations. In both cases, we reported in the morning and started preparing ourselves for our moves.

The first time I went through out-processing in Fort Drum, it was a lot less work. I got to skip a lot of the steps because I wasn't leaving the Army, I was just leaving post. It made it a lot easier. This time, there was twice as much stuff that I had to accomplish before I left. At the time, the Army had to make sure that I wouldn't be homeless when I left the service, so I had to find a place to live before I left. I wasn't going to stay in Colorado Springs, so we found a place to live in Loveland, Colorado. I was going to take a little time off and Paula was going to go back to work. I finished my out-processing, and we loaded up our vehicles to go to our new home and our new life in Northern Colorado.

I got out of the Army in March of 2004. I didn't get choked up leaving this time, probably because I knew I would be coming back to Fort Carson once in a while to see friends. Still, I took the long way out of town to look at it again, just in case something happened and I never made it back.

I asked Paula to marry me when I had gotten out of the service and she said yes. We were married on September 18th, 2004. A little over three years later we would have our daughter. This was my second daughter. I had an older daughter who was born in 2000. These three girls were, and are, my reason for living and always will be.

I went back to school in December of 2004 and attended Regis University through my MBA in 2012. We moved to Cheyenne, Wyoming in 2005 and have resided here ever since. I like living here because I feel right at home with all the Air Force service men and women here. I get to hear aircraft fly over all the time and I get to spend time with my family. Over the years, I have gotten involved with Veterans programs and continue to support our military whenever I can. I am always watching the news to follow what is going on in the world, but I get to do it in a better frame of mind because I know I will not be going if something happens. Even though that does hurt me occasionally, I would do more harm than good for my fellow troops now.

* * *

I suffer from PTSD (Post Traumatic Stress Disorder), I have degenerative discs in my back, my knees are shot, and I'll never be able to run again like I once did. I wake up in pain every day from the time I spent in the service of our country. Along with other health issues, I have constant pain in most of my body. To be clear, I am not complaining about any of this, I am thankful for it. I have a reminder every day for what I was able to do for my country, and for my family. I will always love the military and I will support fellow service members whenever I can.

This book and the rest of my life are dedicated to my family, our country, and all others who serve their fellow men and women in any capacity.